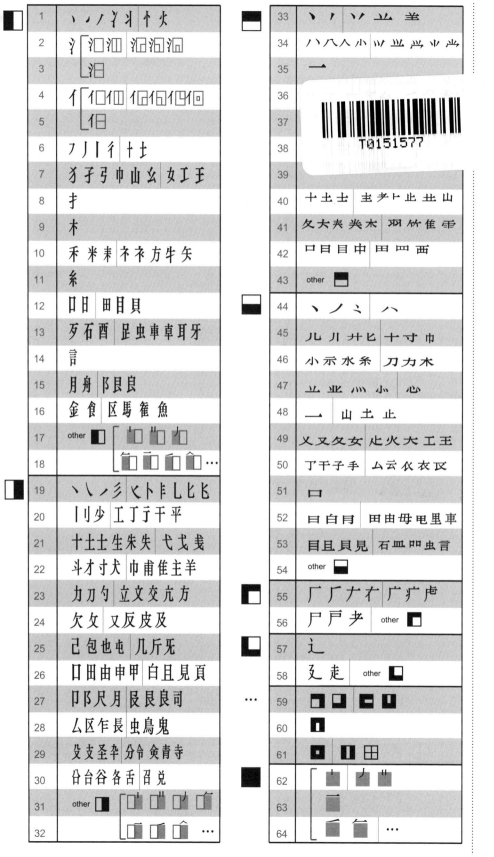

Japanese Kanji

Fast Finder

Laurence Matthews

TUTTLE Publishing

Tokyo | Rutland, Vermont | Singapore

To Alison – for everything

Published by Tuttle Publishing, an imprint of Periplus Editions (HK) Ltd.

www.tuttlepublishing.com

LCC Card No.: 2003110210

ISBN: 978-4-8053-1445-6

ABOUT TUTTLE
"Books to Span the East and West"

Our core mission at Tuttle Publishing is to create books which bring people together one page at a time. Tuttle was founded in 1832 in the small New England town of Rutland, Vermont (USA). Our fundamental values remain as strong today as they were then—to publish best-in-class books informing the English-speaking world about the countries and peoples of Asia. The world has become a smaller place today and Asia's economic, cultural and political influence has expanded, yet the need for meaningful dialogue and information about this diverse region has never been greater. Since 1948, Tuttle has been a leader in publishing books on the cultures, arts, cuisines, languages and literatures of Asia. Our authors and photographers have won numerous awards and Tuttle has published thousands of books on subjects ranging from martial arts to paper crafts. We welcome you to explore the wealth of information available on Asia at www.tuttlepublishing.com.

Distributed by:

North America, Latin America & Europe
Tuttle Publishing
364 Innovation Drive
North Clarendon, VT 05759-9436, USA
Tel: 1 (802) 773 8930
Fax: 1 (802) 773 6993
info@tuttlepublishing.com
www.tuttlepublishing.com

Japan
Tuttle Publishing
Yaekari Building 3rd Floor
5-4-12 Osaki Shinagawa-ku
Tokyo 141 0032 Japan
Tel: (81) 3 5437 0171
Fax: (81) 3 5437 0755
sales@tuttle.co.jp
www.tuttle.co.jp

Asia-Pacific
Berkeley Books Pte Ltd
61 Tai Seng Avenue, #02-12
Singapore 534167
Tel: (65) 6280 1330
Fax: (65) 6280 6290
inquiries@periplus.com.sg
www.periplus.com

Indonesia
PT Java Books Indonesia
Jl. Rawa Gelam IV No.9
Kawasan Industri Pulogadung
Jakarta 13930, Indonesia
Tel: (62) 21 4682 1088
Fax: (62) 21 461 0206
crm@periplus.co.id
www.periplus.com

22 21 20 19 18   10 9 8 7 6 5 4 3 2 1   1806RR
Printed in China

INTRODUCTION

Kanji (Japanese characters) are fascinating, but can be frustrating. In particular, looking up kanji in a traditional dictionary can be a nightmare as there is no "alphabetical order."

With this book you can find a kanji in seconds from its appearance alone. From the finder chart inside the front cover, you can turn to the correct page immediately, and finding the kanji on that page has also been made as simple as possible. As an optional feature you can make a double thumbnail index (see page viii) to speed things up even more.

The Fast Finder is designed primarily for serious learners of kanji and serves as a quick reference for experts, but it is also suitable for beginners, or people who wish to dip into kanji, browse, or simply discover what a street sign means.

With this book you can:

- Find kanji quickly, reliably and intuitively—from their visual appearance alone;
- Quickly check the meanings, readings, stroke-counts and radicals of kanji;
- Look up newly encountered kanji or check ones you have temporarily forgotten;
- Track down elusive kanji more easily than in large kanji dictionaries;
- Simply browse and explore, comparing similar kanji.

There are some hints on finding kanji on page vii, but the system is so intuitive that you can try it right now: for example, try finding 独 or 空. By the time you have looked up half a dozen kanji, you will appreciate the speed with which you can locate kanji in the Fast Finder.

I wish you success, fun and enjoyment in your study of kanji. Ganbatte kudasai!

Kanji

Although many thousands of kanji exist, the Japanese Ministry of Education has designated an official set of 1,945 *jōyō* (general use) kanji. You will see other characters around, particularly those used for names, but these *jōyō* kanji, together with numbers, punctuation and the *hiragana* and *katakana* alphabets (see inside the back cover), essentially constitute the everyday modern Japanese writing system. This book contains all the *jōyō* kanji.

Traditional dictionaries use a system of kanji components called "radicals" to classify kanji. Unfortunately, this system has many pitfalls for the beginner (and even for native speakers of the language!). Thus most dictionaries and kanji guides have indexes ordering the kanji by stroke-count (number of pen-strokes needed to write the kanji) and by reading (pronunciation). However a stroke-count index is slow and unpredictable to use, and a reading index is no help if you don't already know the reading of the kanji. Various systems have been devised to help with this problem: all of them associate codes (such as 2f6.4 or 1-4-2 or 3.1/3) with kanji—and most such systems depend on stroke-counting. This book arose out of my own frustration with these methods when learning kanji, and uses instead the human brain's pattern-recognition abilities directly.

The radical system is basically a good one, but not as logical as one might hope, and experts tend to forget how difficult it was to master the radical system initially. The Fast Finder uses "intuitive radicals": kanji components which you think *ought* to be radicals are treated as such. Most symbols in the finder chart *are* forms of the traditional radicals, though, and so as you use the Fast Finder you will become more familiar with radicals and their quirks, and this will smooth your way to using the many books and dictionaries which are based on the traditional radicals.

Information given

The purpose of this book is to *find* kanji quickly, and to this end the amount of clutter on each page has been kept to a minimum. Thus the information given for each kanji is basic. However, the information is sufficient to determine the meaning of a kanji, to check at a glance any kanji you have confused or temporarily forgotten, or to look up the kanji quickly in your favorite dictionary or kanji guide for fuller information.

Below each kanji are five lines of information. The first two lines give the basic meaning(s) of the kanji and are meant to be read together; if only one line is needed then the second line simply has the symbol "–" For more on meanings, see page x.

The third line gives the kanji's *on* reading (Chinese-derived pronunciation) in capital letters, and the fourth line gives the kanji's *kun* reading (native Japanese pronunciation) in lower case letters. Readings are separated by spaces if the kanji has more than one. All officially approved readings are given. The symbol "#" means that the kanji has no (approved) *on* (or *kun*) reading, and "–" indicates a prefix or suffix. For more on readings, especially the notation used for *kun* readings, see page xi.

The last line of information for each kanji gives its "official" radical and stroke-count. Radicals are listed in Table 1 at the back of the book. In most cases the radical given is the traditional radical, but in a few cases, for historical reasons, the traditional radical is misleading or confusing, and dictionaries differ in their views about which radical to use instead. In these cases an asterisk "*" follows the radical number, the radical listed is that used in the *New Nelson Kanji Dictionary*, and the traditional radical and alternatives are given in Table 2 inside the back cover.

The stroke-count of the kanji will help you to look up the kanji in the stroke-count index of a large dictionary (although using a reading index is easier, if there is one), and will also be of use if you are using a dictionary based on stroke-count of kanji components. The stroke count for most kanji is universally agreed, but unfortunately in a (very) few cases dictionaries will disagree on stroke-count too.

Hints on finding kanji

It is a good idea to look through the book to get a feel for how the kanji are organised and displayed. The Fast Finder is organised with many kanji to a page, so that you can see at a glance the kanji which share a particular radical – and you can profitably browse this way too.

Dividing up a kanji

Initially you might find you have a tendency to regard any kanji which doesn't split left-right as indivisible; but you will see that the kanji on pages 62-64 (the "indivisible" kanji) are generally quite simple ones. The vast majority of kanji do divide into components.

To find a specific kanji, first look at how it naturally breaks down into components. Having split the kanji, choose the simpler component as your radical, which you will use to look up the kanji. If the components look roughly equal in simplicity, choose either; if you already recognise one of the components as a radical, you can use that. The same kanji may be found in two places: for example you will find 引 under ■ on page 7, and also under ▊ on page 20.

In fact many kanji are to be found in several different locations in the Fast Finder. A consequence of having compact information for each kanji is that the whole entry can be repeated in each of these locations, thus eliminating the need for cross-references, and avoiding any need to decide which radical is "correct."

Although most kanji split left-right or top-bottom, don't forget the other patterns (pages 55-61). For these kanji, use the enclosing component as the radical.

Sometimes there is a choice of how much of the kanji to take as the radical. For example, when looking for 畑, is the radical ⺀ or 火? In most such cases, both radicals will be on the same page to make it easier to find the kanji (in odd cases where they are not, then the kanji will be found in both places). Kanji with several reasonable lookup methods are listed under all of these. But I rely on you not to make "unnatural" divisions: 聖 is in the ▬ section under 耳, not 土.

Finally, if looking for a kanji which also serves as a radical, treat it as a kanji in its own right. For example, you would look up 鐘 under ▮ on page 16, but 金 itself under ▬ on page 34.

Finding the right page

Look for your radical in the finder chart inside the front cover. Remember to look in the correct section of the finder chart (▮ or ▮ , etc.) as several radicals appear in more than one section. The arrangement of the radicals in the finder chart is intuitive, with similar radicals grouped together, and the simpler ones generally coming before the complex ones. If you can't find the radical in the finder chart, look on the relevant "others" page (these are pages such as 17, 18 and 43, and contain the radicals which have only one or two kanji each). You will very quickly become familiar with the common radicals, which appear explicitly in the finder chart, and hence sense when to look on the "others" pages.

As illustrated on the inside front cover, if a radical has many kanji then they will be subdivided according to how the remainder of the kanji divides up. In the case of two particularly common radicals which flow onto two pages (pages 2-3 and 4-5), this idea is used in the finder chart too.

For "indivisible" kanji, the shape of the top of the kanji is used; you can see how this works by glancing through pages 62-64. The same idea is used for the "others" pages and implicitly elsewhere.

Finding the kanji on the page

When you turn to the correct page, check at the top of the page that your chosen radical is there. (The thin vertical gray lines in the finder chart inside the front cover indicate whether to look on the left hand or right hand page).

The kanji for the same radical are grouped together: again, the arrangement is intuitive with the simpler kanji coming before the more complex. Kanji which are very similar and likely to be confused, such as 何 and 伺, or 殻 and 穀 are placed close together. As above, if a radical has many kanji then they will be arranged according to how the remainder of the kanji divides up.

If the kanji itself is printed in gray, then you were not really looking for it in the right place: never mind, at least you have found it! However, the same kanji will appear elsewhere in the book, printed in black. As you use the Fast Finder, taking a closer look at these gray kanji will help you to appreciate more precisely how kanji components fit together and to distinguish between similar and easily-confused components. You are bound to find some gray kanji where you would not imagine that anyone would look for them, but rest assured that there are people who would, and did!

Important distinctions

If you are new to kanji, then there are several variants to watch for. Make sure you distinguish between radicals such as 亠 and 宀, or 力 and 刀, for example. You will learn these distinctions with time (in fact, pretty quickly).

On the other hand, unfortunately, some variants denote the same kanji. A few kanji have minor variations from one typeface to another, or are slightly different when hand-written, and some slightly older versions of kanji components are still around. For example,

令 is the same as 令 and 曷 is the same as 曷.

Kanji also incorporate relics from much earlier times. For example, many traditional radicals have several forms, depending on whether they appear to the left, right, top, bottom, etc. of the kanji to which they contribute (see Table 1 at the back of the book). Thus:

犭 and 犬 are different forms of the "dog" radical;

忄 and 心 are different forms of the "heart" radical.

To further complicate matters, many of these forms have different stroke-counts, which means that in some dictionaries finding even the radicals is a problem! In the Fast Finder these forms are treated as though they are different radicals, in the general belief that although facts about the kanji and their historical derivations can be fascinating, they should not frustrate your attempts simply to *find* a kanji.

Meanings

The English meanings given are as short and concise as possible; their purpose is to "suggest and remind" as one book puts it. From the meanings given, you will usually be able to deduce the meaning of the kanji in a given context, but note the following points.

Kanji do not usually correspond neatly to single English words. Like an English word, a kanji may have several distinct meanings. (If so, do not assume that the meanings correspond in any one-to-one manner with the readings. A kanji dictionary will make it clear which readings can take which meanings).

Where several meanings are given, similar meanings are separated by commas and distinct meanings by semicolons. If two meanings are separated by commas then they may qualify each other: thus "firm, hard" indicates firm to the touch rather than either industrial organisation or difficult. A particular phrase to note is "state, condition" which is used for a number of kanji meaning state, condition, situation, circumstances (as opposed to provide verbally, nation or proviso). Sometimes a kanji has a huge range of meanings depending on context, and this is indicated by "…"

Conversely, several kanji may share a common English meaning, so be wary of using this book to translate in the English-to-Japanese direction (another issue in this context is honorifics: words such as "give" and "receive" often have connotations of humility or conversely "deigning to" attached to them, which are generally not indicated in the Fast Finder).

Current rather than original meanings are given. The kanji 十 historically meant "needle" but now usually means "ten", so the meaning "needle" is not given.

Meanings given in italics (e.g. *tatami*, *haiku*) are Japanese words: any you don't recognise will often be obsolete units of weights and measures, such as *monme*, *rin*, *shaku*.

Transitive and intransitive verbs, and indeed nouns, verbs, and adjectives, can often be converted easily into each other in Japanese by using different endings to the kanji, which acts like a "stem" in English. For example the kanji 憎, "hate," is used for:

niku*mu*	to hate
niku*i*, niku*rashii*	hateful
niku*shimi*	hatred

where the portions written in italics are grammatical endings spelled out with *hiragana*. (See inside the back cover—and note that many books use parentheses instead of italics, writing niku(mu), etc.) The meaning of the kanji may be given as the noun, the verb, or the adjective: whichever is simplest, clearest, and least ambiguous.

Finally, "counters" are omitted from the meanings listed. Quite a few kanji serve as counting units for nouns, analogous to the word "head" in "six head of cattle." Counters are usually easily recognised in Japanese as they always directly follow numbers.

As far as compounds (words made up of two or more kanji) are concerned, their meanings can be guessed, more often than not, from the context and the meanings of the individual kanji. But of course many derived meanings are somewhat oblique, in the same way that English words such as "laptop" and "honeymoon" have meanings not implicit in their component parts.

Readings

Kanji have two sorts of pronunciations or readings: *on* and *kun* readings. Most kanji have one of each, but many kanji have several; and many others have an *on* reading but no *kun* reading or vice versa.

On readings are derived from Chinese; by and large they are used in compound words consisting of two or more kanji taken together. *Kun* readings are the native Japanese pronunciations of words; they are generally used for kanji which stand alone or with *okurigana* (grammatical endings spelled out in *hiragana*). Thus 車 meaning "vehicle" is pronounced *kuruma* when on its own, but it is pronounced *sha* in a compound like 電車 *densha* which means "train, streetcar." This means that when you are looking for a compound word in an alphabetical-ly-arranged Japanese dictionary, you will tend to be using *on* readings.

All officially approved *on* and *kun* readings are given. However, for clarity and to save space, the full list of possible *okurigana* for each *kun* reading is not given. *Okurigana* are given in italics; the symbol ".." shows that the reading may take other *okurigana* as well. If there are several *kun* readings, *okurigana* for subsequent ones are simply indicated by the symbol "+".

Thus the listing for *niku* (see the previous page) is rendered simply as niku*mu*. In a similar way:

haya*i*, haya*maru*, haya*meru*	becomes	haya*i*..
ashi, ta*ru*, ta*riru*, ta*su*	becomes	ashi, ta+

Providing a kanji has a *kun* reading, the fastest way to locate the kanji in a large kanji dictionary is usually to look up this *kun* reading in the reading index, and for this reason the Fast Finder always provides at least one set of *okurigana* (unless the kanji has a *kun* reading without *okurigana*, like *ashi* above, in which case use that).

Readings sometimes undergo minor changes in compounds (e.g. *–kane* might change to *–gane*), and there are also irregular readings for some compounds. The Fast Finder does not list these variants and irregular readings.

Thumbnail index

A unique feature of the Fast Finder is the option to make a double thumbnail index, as illustrated in the diagram below. This speeds up the use of the Fast Finder even more. This is especially noticeable if you are using it repeatedly to look up many kanji.

The thumbnail index allows immediate access to any page directly from the finder chart inside the front cover. Simply find the desired radical in the finder chart as normal, then put your right thumb on the tab with the chosen page number to open the book at the correct page. This tab will be on the same horizontal line as the radical you have found (so this actually bypasses the need to note the page number).

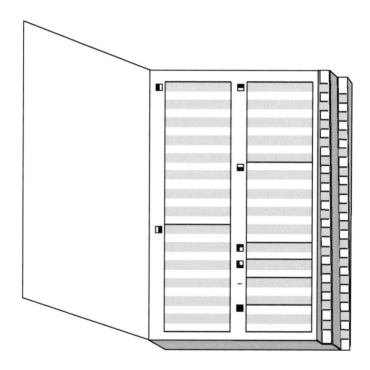

To make the thumbnail index, cut the main pages as indicated by the heavy black lines in the block on the right hand side of each right-hand page, as illustrated in the diagram below:

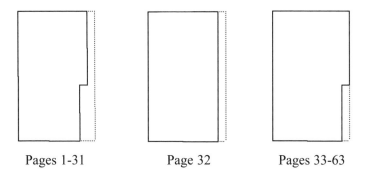

Pages 1-31   Page 32   Pages 33-63

For the main pages it is best to make the horizontal cut first, followed by the vertical cut or cuts. Be careful when cutting the pages to make sure that you are not unintentionally cutting two pages at once.

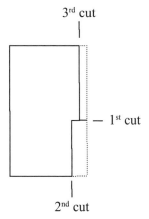

3rd cut

— 1st cut

2nd cut

In order to have the thumbnail index visible from the finder chart, you will also have to cut these introductory pages, including the finder chart itself. Cut along the line marked on the right hand edge of the right hand pages.

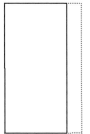

Pages v, vii, ix, xi, xiii

Kanji	Meaning	On-reading	Kun-reading	Radical / Strokes
並	line up; ordinary	HEI	narabu.. nami	r 1* s 8
寸	tiny; -	SUN	#	r 41 s 3
勺	*shaku*; -	SHAKU	#	r 20 s 3
為	do; purpose	I	#	r 86* s 9
氷	ice; -	HYŌ	kōri kō- hi	r 85 s 5
火	fire; Tuesday	KA	hi ho	r 86 s 4
心	heart; -	SHIN	kokoro	r 61 s 4
必	inevitable; -	HITSU	kanarazu	r 61 s 5
州	state, province; sandbank	SHŪ	su	r 47 s 6
帰	return home	KI	kaeru..	r 50* s 10
小	small	SHŌ	chiisai ko- o-	r 42 s 3
少	few	SHŌ	sukoshi suku+	r 42 s 4
劣	inferior	RETSU	otoru	r 19 s 6
省	minister; omit; reflect upon; …	SHŌ SEI	habuku kaeri+	r 109 s 9
次	next; -	JI SHI	tsugi tsu+	r 76 s 6
准	quasi-; semi; ratify	JUN	#	r 15 s 10
凍	freeze; -	TŌ	kōru kogo+	r 15 s 10
冷	cold; -	REI	tsumetai hi+ sa+	r 15 s 7
凝	stiff; elaborate	GYŌ	koru..	r 15 s 16
求	seek, request	KYŪ	motomeru	r 85 s 7
兆	sign, omen; trillion	CHŌ	kizashi..	r 10 s 6
羽	feather, wing	U	ha hane	r 124 s 6
弱	weak; -	JAKU	yowai..	r 57 s 10
症	symptoms; -	SHŌ	#	r 104 s 10
疾	disease; speed	SHITSU	#	r 104 s 10
疲	fatigue; -	HI	tsukareru..	r 104 s 10
病	illness; -	BYŌ HEI	yamai ya+	r 104 s 10
疫	epidemic; -	EKI YAKU	#	r 104 s 9
痘	smallpox; -	TŌ	#	r 104 s 12
痛	pain; -	TSŪ	itamu..	r 104 s 12
痢	diarrhea; -	RI	#	r 104 s 12
痴	foolish; -	CHI	#	r 104 s 13
癖	habit; -	HEKI	kuse	r 104 s 18
癒	heal; -	YU	iya+ ie+	r 104 s 18
療	treat illness; -	RYŌ	#	r 104 s 17
壮	grand, strong	SŌ	#	r 32* s 6
状	letter; state, condition	JŌ	#	r 94 s 7
将	leader; soon	SHŌ	#	r 41 s 10
北	north; -	HOKU	kita	r 21 s 5
兆	sign, omen; trillion	CHŌ	kizashi..	r 10 s 6

忙 busy - BŌ isoga*shii* r 61 s 6	快 pleasant - KAI kokoroyo*i* r 61 s 7	性 sex; nature, essence - SEI SHŌ # r 61 s 8	怖 fear - FU kowa*i* r 61 s 8	恨 grudge; regret KON ura*mu*.. r 61 s 9	
悼 mourn - TŌ ita*mu* r 61 s 11	慎 discreet - SHIN tsutsushi*mu* r 61 s 13	憤 indignant - FUN ikidō*ru* r 61 s 15	懐 bosom; yearn for KAI futokoro natsu+ r 61 s 16	憶 guess; recollect OKU # r 61 s 16	情 emotion; state, condition JŌ SEI nasa*ke* r 61 s 11
惜 regret - SEKI o*shii*.. r 61 s 11	慌 flustered - KŌ awa*teru*.. r 61 s 12	悦 joy - ETSU # r 61 s 10	憎 hate - ZŌ niku*mu*.. r 61 s 14	悩 anguish, distress NŌ naya*mu*.. r 61 s 10	惰 lazy - DA # r 61 s 12
恒 constant - KŌ # r 61 s 9	怪 strange, weird, spooky KAI aya*shii*.. r 61 s 8	悟 enlightened - GO sato*ru* r 61 s 10	慢 arrogant; lazy MAN # r 61 s 14	慣 accustomed - KAN na*reru*.. r 61 s 14	悔 repent - KAI kui*ru*.. kuya+ r 61 s 9
惨 cruel; miserable SAN ZAN mije*me* r 61 s 11	愉 pleasure - YU # r 61 s 12	憾 regret - KAN # r 61 s 16			
慨 deplore - GAI # r 61 s 13	怖 fear - FU kowa*i* r 61 s 8				
灯 lamp - TŌ hi r 86 s 6	炊 cook, boil SUI ta*ku* r 86 s 8	炉 furnace, hearth RO # r 86 s 8	畑 field - # hata hatake r 102 s 9	煩 trouble, worry HAN BON wazura*u*.. r 86 s 13	煙 smoke - EN kemuri kemu+ r 86 s 13
燥 dry - SŌ # r 86 s 17	焼 burn, bake SHŌ ya*keru*.. r 86 s 12	爆 explode - BAKU # r 86 s 19	燃 burn, combust NEN mo*eru*.. r 86 s 16		

■▯ 氵 氵

汁	汗	江	沖	決	沈
juice, soup	sweat	inlet, river	open sea	decide	sink (into)
JŪ	- KAN	KŌ	- CHŪ	- KETSU	- CHIN
shiru	ase	e	oki	ki*meru*..	shizu*mu*..
r 85 s 5	r 85 s 6	r 85 s 6	r 85 s 7	r 85 s 7	r 85 s 7

池	泌	泣	汚
pond	secrete	weep, cry	dirty
- CHI	- HITSU HI	KYŪ	- O
ike	#	na*ku*	kitana*i* kega+ yogo+
r 85 s 6	r 85 s 8	r 85 s 6	r 85 s 8

油	活	酒
oil	active	rice wine, *sake*
- YU	- KATSU	SHU
abura	#	sake saka-
r 85 s 8	r 85 s 9	r 164 s 10

沸	浄	津	浅	浦
boiling	pure	harbor; ferry	shallow	bay; shore
- FUTSU	- JŌ	SHIN	- SEN	- HO
wa*ku*..	#	tsu	asa*i*	ura
r 85 s 8	r 85 s 9	r 85 s 9	r 85 s 9	r 85 s 10

測	湖	潮	漸	瀬
measure	lake	tide; seawater	gradually	shallows, rapids
- SOKU	- KO	CHŌ	- ZEN	#
haka*ru*	mizuumi	shio	#	se
r 85 s 12	r 85 s 12	r 85 s 15	r 85 s 14	r 85 s 19

淑	激
graceful	violent
- SHUKU	- GEKI
#	hage*shii*
r 85 s 11	r 85 s 16

沢	泥	涙	漏	
marsh; plenty; ...	mud	tears	leak	
-	-	-	-	
TAKU	DEI	RUI	RŌ	
sawa	doro	namida	mo*ru*..	
r 85 s 7	r 85 s 8	r 85 s 10	r 85 s 14	

派	涯	源	波	渡
faction; send	limit, edge	source	waves	cross over
HA	GAI	-	-	TO
#	#	GEN	HA	
		minamoto	nami	wata*ru*..
r 85 s 9	r 85 s 11	r 85 s 13	r 85 s 8	r 85 s 12

河	泡	減	滅	
river	bubbles	decrease	perish; destroy	
-	-	-	METSU	
KA	HŌ	GEN	horo*biru*..	
kawa	awa	he*ru*		
r 85 s 8	r 85 s 8	r 85 s 12	r 85 s 13	

洞	潤	減	滅	滴
cave	moisten	decrease	perish; destroy	drip
-	-	-	METSU	-
DŌ	JUN	GEN	horo*biru*..	TEKI
hora	uruo*u*.. uru+	he*ru*		shizuku shitata+
r 85 s 9	r 85 s 15	r 85 s 12	r 85 s 13	r 85 s 14

■ 泊：泊 泊 泊 泊 泊

泊

泣	済	涼	流	液	湾
weep, cry	settle up; finish	cool	current; style	fluid	bay
KYŪ	SAI	RYŌ	RYŪ RU	EKI	WAN
na*ku*	su*mu*..	suzu*shii*..	naga*reru*..	#	#
r 85 s 8	r 85 s 11	r 85 s 11	r 85 s 10	r 85 s 11	r 85 s 12

法	溶	演	滝	滴	
law; method	melt, dissolve	performance	waterfall	drip	
HŌ HA' HO'	YŌ	EN	#	TEKI	
#	to*keru*..	#	taki	shizuku shitata+	
r 85 s 8	r 85 s 13	r 85 s 14	r 85 s 13	r 85 s 14	

洗	清	漬	漆	淡	消
wash	pure	pickle	lacquer	faint, light, pale	extinguish; consume
SEN	SEI SHŌ	#	SHITSU	TAN	SHŌ
ara*u*	kiyo*i*..	tsu*keru*..	urushi	awa*i*	ke*su* ki+
r 85 s 9	r 85 s 11	r 85 s 14	r 85 s 14	r 85 s 11	r 85 s 10

泊

洪	港	漠	満	漢	溝
flood	harbor, port	vague; vast	full	Chinese	ditch
KŌ	KŌ	BAKU	MAN	KAN	KŌ
#	minato	#	mi*tasu*..	#	mizo
r 85 s 9	r 85 s 12	r 85 s 13	r 85 s 12	r 85 s 13	r 85 s 13

濃	渋	渉	滞		
dense, thick, deep	astringent; hesitant	ford; connect	stay, stagnate		
NŌ	JŪ	SHŌ	TAI		
Ko*i*	shibu*i*..	#	todokō*ru*		
r 85 s 16	r 85 s 11	r 85 s 11	r 85 s 13		

泊
泊
泊

注	泳	浅	浦	泊	浪
pour; take note	swim	shallow	bay; shore	overnight	waves; roam
CHŪ	EI	SEN	HO	HAKU	RŌ
soso*gu*	oyo*gu*	asa*i*	ura	to*maru*..	#
r 85 s 8	r 85 s 8	r 85 s 9	r 85 s 10	r 85 s 8	r 85 s 10

泊

洋	滋	消			
ocean; Western	nourish; moist	extinguish; consume			
YŌ	JI	SHŌ			
#	#	ke*su* ki+			
r 85 s 9	r 85 s 12	r 85 s 10			

泪

涙 tears - RUI namida r 85 s 10	酒 rice wine, sake SHU sake saka- r 164 s 10	添 add to - TEN soeru.. r 85 s 11	漂 drift - HYŌ tadayou r 85 s 14	況 conditions - KYŌ # r 85 s 8	
湿 damp - SHITSU shimeru.. r 85 s 12	湯 hot water - TŌ yu r 85 s 12	渇 thirst - KATSU kawaku r 85 s 11	混 mix - KON mazeru.. r 85 s 11	温 warm - ON atatakai.. r 85 s 12	漫 aimless; comic MAN # r 85 s 14
沼 marsh - SHŌ numa r 85 s 8	浸 soak - SHIN hitaru.. r 85 s 10	没 sink; die; disappear BOTSU # r 85 s 7	濁 muddy - DAKU nigoru.. r 85 s 16	滑 slide; smooth KATSU suberu name+ r 85 s 13	渦 whirlpool - KA uzu r 85 s 12

泪

活 active - KATSU # r 85 s 9	浜 beach - HIN hama r 85 s 10	浮 floating - FU ukabu.. r 85 s 10	渓 ravine - KEI # r 85 s 11

泪

汽 steam - KI # r 85 s 7	深 deep - SHIN fukai.. r 85 s 11	海 sea - KAI umi r 85 s 9	浄 fishing - GYO RYŌ # r 85 s 14

…

沿 along - EN sou r 85 s 8	浴 bathe - YOKU abiru.. r 85 s 10	治 govern; heal JI CHI naoru.. osa+ r 85 s 8	潟 lagoon - # kata r 85 s 15

泪

濯 wash, rinse TAKU # r 85 s 17	濫 excessive - RAN # r 85 s 18	潔 pure - KETSU isagiyoi r 85 s 15	潜 submerge; hide, lurk SEN moguru hiso+ r 85 s 15	澄 clear - CHŌ sumu.. r 85 s 15	潟 lagoon - # kata r 85 s 15

1	33
2	34
3	35
4	36
5	37
6	38
7	39
8	40
9	41
10	42
11	43
12	44
13	45
14	46
15	47
16	48
17	49
18	50
19	51
20	52
21	53
22	54
23	55
24	56
25	57
26	58
27	59
28	60
29	61
30	62
31	63
32	64

■ 仃 仢

仏	化	他	仙	作	
Buddha; France	transform	other	hermit; fairy	make	
BUTSU	- KA KE	- TA	SEN	SAKU SA	
hotoke	bake*ru*..	#	#	tsuku*ru*	
r 9 s 4	r 21 s 4	r 9 s 5	r 9 s 5	r 9 s 7	

付	代	伐	伏		
attach	replace; era; price	cut down	prostrate; ambush		
FU	DAI TAI	BATSU	FUKU		
tsuku*ku*..	shiro ka+ yo	#	fu*u*..		
r 9 s 5	r 9 s 5	r 9 s 6	r 9 s 6		

仕	休	体	件	伴	
serve	rest	body	affair	accompany	
- SHI JI	- KYŪ	TAI TEI	KEN	HAN BAN	
tsuka*eru*	yasu*mu*..	karada	#	tomona*u*	
r 9 s 5	r 9 s 6	r 9* s 7	r 9 s 6	r 9 s 7	

位	依	任	住	伯	偽
rank; approx.	rely on	entrust; duties	dwell	aunt, uncle; earl	deceive, forgery
I	- I E	NIN	- JŪ	HAKU	GI
kurai	#	maka*seru*..	su*mu*..	#	nise itsuwa+
r 9 s 7	r 9 s 8	r 9 s 6	r 9 s 7	r 9 s 7	r 9 s 11

仲	伸	使	便	価	信
relationship	extend, stretch	use; envoy	handy; mail; excreta	price, value	trust; letter
- CHŪ	SHIN	SHI	BIN BEN	KA	SHIN
naka	no*biru*..	tsuka*u*	tayori	atai	#
r 9 s 6	r 9 s 7	r 9 s 8	r 9 s 9	r 9 s 8	r 9 s 9

似	仰	俳	候	修	傾
resemble	look up at; respect	*haiku*; actor	season; climate	learn; mend	inclination
- JI	GYŌ KŌ	HAI	KŌ	SHŪ SHU	- KEI
ni*ru*	ao*gu* ō+	#	sōrō	osa*meru*..	katamu*ku*..
r 9 s 7	r 9 s 10	r 9 s 10	r 9 s 10	r 9 s 10	r 9 s 13

倣	側	例	倒	働	
imitate	side	example	topple; inverted	work	
HŌ	SOKU	- REI	TŌ	- DŌ	
nara*u*	kawa	tato*eru*	tao*reru*	hatara*ku*	
r 9 s 10	r 9 s 11	r 9 s 8	r 9 s 10	r 9 s 13	

佀 佀 佀 佀

佀

佐	仮	偏	備
assistant	temporary	leaning, bias	equip, provide
-	-	HEN	BI
SA	KA KE	katayo*ru*	sona*eru*
#	kari	r 9 s 11	r 9 s 12
r 9 s 7	r 9 s 6		

佀

何	伺
what, how many	visit; pay respects
KA	SHI
nani nan	ukaga*u*
r 9 s 7	r 9 s 7

佀

値	健
value, price	healthy
CHI	-
ne atai	KEN
r 9 s 10	suko*yaka*
	r 9 s 11

佀

個
individual; item
KO
#
r 9 s 10

1	33
2	34
3	35
4	36
5	37
6	38
7	39
8	40
9	41
10	42
11	43
12	44
13	45
14	46
15	47
16	48
17	49
18	50
19	51
20	52
21	53
22	54
23	55
24	56
25	57
26	58
27	59
28	60
29	61
30	62
31	63
32	64

■ 伯 ： 伯 佮 伯 伯 佮

伯

佳	侍	俵	債	停
excellent	*samurai*; serve	bag, sack	debt	stop
-	JI	HYŌ	SAI	TEI
KA	samurai	tawara	#	#
#				
r 9　s 8	r 9　s 8	r 9　s 10	r 9　s 13	r 9　s 11

依	位	倍	億	傍	僚
rely on	rank; approx.	multiple, -fold	100 million	beside	colleague; official
I E	I	BAI	OKU	BŌ	RYŌ
#	kurai	#	#	kataw*ara*	#
r 9　s 8	r 9　s 7	r 9　s 10	r 9　s 15	r 9　s 12	r 9　s 14

偵	偉	催	俸
spy	eminent	sponsor, organise	salary
-	-	SAI	-
TEI	er*ai*	moyō*su*	HŌ
#			#
r 9　s 11	r 9　s 12	r 9　s 13	r 9　s 10

佮

供	借	僕
offer	borrow, rent	I (male); servant
-	SHAKU	BOKU
KYŌ KU	ka*riru*	#
tomo sona+		
r 9　s 8	r 9　s 10	r 9　s 14

伯 伯

住	偽	伯
dwell	deceive, forgery	aunt, uncle; earl
-	GI	HAKU
JŪ	nise itsuwa+	#
su*mu*..		
r 9　s 7	r 9　s 11	r 9　s 7

佮

併	僧	儀	償
combine, unite	priest; monk	ceremony	compensate
HEI	SŌ	GI	SHŌ
awa*seru*	#	#	tsuguna*u*
r 9　s 8	r 9　s 13	r 9　s 15	r 9　s 17

佰

仁	伝	信	偏
compassion	transmit	trust; letter	leaning, bias
-	-	-	-
JIN NI	DEN	SHIN	HEN
#	tsuta*eru*..	#	katayo*ru*
r9 s4	r9 s6	r9 s9	r9 s11

価	便	儒	優
price, value	handy; mail; excreta	Confucian	cordial; excel; actor
KA	BIN BEN	-	YŪ
atai	tayori	JU	sugu*reru* yasa+
r9 s8	r9 s9	# r9 s16	r9 s17

但	保	促	偶
however; proviso	preserve	urge on	by chance; couple; doll
#	-	-	GŪ
tada*shi*	HO tamotsu	SOKU unaga*su*	#
r9 s7	r9 s9	r9 s9	r9 s11

侯	侵
marquis	invade
-	-
KŌ	SHIN
#	oka*su*
r9 s9	r9 s9

佰

任	低	係
entrust; duties	low	in charge; link
NIN	-	KEI
maka*seru*..	TEI hiku*i*..	kakari kaka+
r9 s6	r9 s7	r9 s9

佰

侮	傷	像
scorn	wound	image
-	-	-
BU	SHŌ	ZŌ
anado*ru*	kizu ita+	#
r9 s8	r9 s13	r9 s14

…

俗	倹	倫	俊
vulgar; custom	thrifty	ethics	genius
ZOKU	-	-	-
#	KEN	RIN	SHUN
r9 s9	#	#	#
	r9 s10	r9 s10	r9 s9

佃

傑
outstanding
-
KETSU
#
r9 s13

1	33
2	34
3	35
4	36
5	37
6	38
7	39
8	40
9	41
10	42
11	43
12	44
13	45
14	46
15	47
16	48
17	49
18	50
19	51
20	52
21	53
22	54
23	55
24	56
25	57
26	58
27	59
28	60
29	61
30	62
31	63
32	64

ﾌ ﾉ | ｲ

承	水	永	氷	
Consent, be told	water; Wednesday	eternal	ice	
SHŌ	SUI	- EI	HYŌ	
uketamawaru	mizu	nagai	kōri kō- hi	
r 64 s 8	r 85 s 4	r 85 s 5	r 85 s 5	

八	川	順	入	粛
eight	river	sequence; obey	enter; put in, let in	solemn; purge
- HACHI	- SEN	JUN	NYŪ	SHUKU
ya ya'+ ya+ yō	kawa	#	hairu i+	#
r 12 s 2	r 47 s 3	r 181 s 12	r 11 s 2	r 129 s 11

旧	以
old, former	by means of; datum
KYŪ	I
#	#
r 72* s 5	r 9 s 5

行	往	従	征	律	彼
go; do; line	go; bygone	follow	conquer; go to war	law; rhythm	he, she, they; that (yonder)
GYŌ KŌ AN	Ō	- JŪ JU SHŌ	SEI	RITSU RICHI	HI
iku yu+ okona+	#	shitagau..	#	#	kare kano
r 144 s 6	r 60 s 8	r 60 s 10	r 60 s 8	r 60 s 9	r 60 s 8

待	徒	徳	復	後	
await	futile; walk; follower	virtue	restore, re-	after	
- TAI	TO	- TOKU	FUKU	- GO KŌ	
matsu	#	#	#	nochi ushi+ ushiro ato oku+	
r 60 s 9	r 60 s 10	r 60 s 14	r 60 s 12	r 60 s 9	

得	役	径	徐	循	
gain	service, duty	path; diameter	slowly	circulate	
- TOKU	EKI YAKU	KEI	- JO	- JUN	
eru u+	#	#	#	#	
r 60 s 11	r 60 s 7	r 60 s 8	r 60 s 10	r 60 s 12	

街	術	衡	衝	衛	
street, arcade	art, skill	balance, scales	collide	guard	
GAI KAI	JUTSU	KŌ	- SHŌ	EI	
machi	#	#	#	#	
r 60* s 12	r 60* s 11	r 60* s 16	r 60* s 15	r 60* s 16	

徴	微	徹	御	
symptom; levy	tiny, faint, hard to see	thorough	(honorific); control	
CHŌ	BI	- TETSU	GYO GO	
#	#	#	on-	
r 60 s 14	r 60 s 13	r 60 s 15	r 60 s 12	

1	33
2	34
3	35
4	36
5	37
6	38
7	39
8	40
9	41
10	42
11	43
12	44
13	45
14	46
15	47
16	48
17	49
18	50
19	51
20	52
21	53
22	54
23	55
24	56
25	57
26	58
27	59
28	60
29	61
30	62
31	63
32	64

† ±

協
co-operate
-
KYŌ
#
r 24 s 8

博
extensive;
Dr; gamble; ...
HAKU BAKU
#
r 24 s 12

雄
male;
brave
YŪ
osu o
r 172 s 12

地
earth, ground;
place
CHI JI
#
r 32 s 6

坪
tsubo;
floor area
#
tsubo
r 32 s 8

坑
pit
-
KŌ
#
r 32 s 7

坊
boy;
priest
BŌ BO'
#
r 32 s 7

培
cultivate
-
BAI
tsuchikau
r 32 s 11

境
border;
state, condition
KYŌ KEI
sakai
r 32 s 14

壊
demolish
-
KAI
kowareru..
r 32 s 16

壌
soil,
earth
JŌ
#
r 32 s 16

墳
tumulus
-
FUN
#
r 32 s 15

壇
podium
-
DAN TAN
#
r 32 s 16

塔
tower
-
TŌ
#
r 32 s 12

堪
endure
-
KAN
taeru
r 32 s 12

塊
lump
-
KAI
katamari
r 32 s 13

増
increase
-
ZŌ
masu fu+
r 32 s 14

垣
fence
-
#
kaki
r 32 s 9

埋
bury
-
MAI
umeru..
r 32 s 10

堤
embankment
-
TEI
tsutsumi
r 32 s 12

場
place,
location
JŌ
ba
r 32 s 12

塩
salt
-
EN
shio
r 32* s 13

塚
mound
-
#
tsuka
r 32 s 12

坂
slope
-
HAN
saka
r 32 s 7

塀
fence,
wall
HEI
#
r 32 s 12

堀
ditch
-
#
hori
r 32 s 11

均
equal
-
KIN
#
r 32 s 7

域
area,
zone
IKI
#
r 32 s 11

城
castle
-
JŌ
shiro
r 32 s 9

犭

犯	狂	独	狭	狩	猛
crime	mad	alone; Germany	narrow	hunt	fierce
-	-	-	-	-	-
HAN	KYŌ	DOKU	KYŌ	SHU	MŌ
oka*su*	kuru*u..*	hito*ri*	sema*i* seba+	ka*ru..*	#
r 94 s 5	r 94 s 7	r 94 s 9	r 94 s 9	r 94 s 9	r 94 s 11

猫	猟	猶	獲	猿	獄
cat	hunting	delay; yet, still	capture	monkey	prison
-	-	-	-	-	-
BYŌ	RYŌ	YŪ	KAKU	EN	GOKU
neko	#	#	e*ru*	saru	#
r 94 s 11	r 94 s 11	r 94 s 12	r 94 s 16	r 94 s 13	r 94 s 14

子

孔	孤	孫
hole	solitary, orphan	grandchild
-	-	-
KŌ	KO	SON
#	#	mago
r 39 s 4	r 39 s 8	r 39 s 10

弓

引	弦	強	弧	張	弾
pull	string (eg of bow, harp)	strong	arc, arch	stretch	bullet; play (eg harp); …
-	-	-	-	-	-
IN	GEN	KYŌ GŌ	KO	CHŌ	DAN
hi*ku..*	tsuru	tsuyo*i..* shi+	#	ha*ru*	tama hazu+ hi+
r 57 s 4	r 57 s 8	r 57 s 11	r 57 s 9	r 57 s 11	r 57 s 12

巾

帆	帳	幅	帽
sail	notebook; curtain	width, breadth	hat
-	-	-	-
HAN	CHŌ	FUKU	BŌ
ho	#	haba	#
r 50 s 6	r 50 s 11	r 50 s 12	r 50 s 12

山

岬	岐	峡	崎	峰	峠
headland, cape	diverge	ravine	headland, cape	summit	mountain pass
#	-	-	#	-	#
misaki	KI	KYŌ	saki	HŌ	tōge
r 46 s 8	#	#	r 46 s 11	mine	r 46 s 9
	r 46 s 7	r 46 s 9		r 46 s 10	

幺

幻	幼	郷
illusion	infant	hometown; rural
-	-	KYŌ GŌ
GEN	YŌ	#
maboroshi	osana*i*	r 163 s 11
r 52 s 4	r 52 s 5	

■□ 女 工 王

妃	queen, empress / HI / # / r 38 s 6
奴	slave; guy / DO NU / # / r 38 s 5
如	as, like, such as / JO NYO / # / r 38 s 6
好	good; fond of / KŌ / kono*mu* su+ / r 38 s 6
妊	pregnant / NIN / # / r 38 s 7

妹	younger sister / MAI / imōto / r 38 s 8
姓	surname / SEI SHŌ / # / r 38 s 8
始	begin / SHI / haji*maru*.. / r 38 s 8
娘	daughter / - / # / musume / r 38 s 10
妨	obstruct / BŌ / samata*geru* / r 38 s 7
姉	elder sister / SHI / ane / r 38 s 8

妙	miraculous; odd / MYŌ / # / r 38 s 7
嫁	bride; marry (a man) / KA / yome totsu+ / r 38 s 13
嫡	legitimate heir / CHAKU / # / r 38 s 14
嬢	girl / - / JŌ / # / r 38 s 16
嫌	dislike / KEN GEN / kira*u iya* / r 38 s 13
媒	mediation / BAI / # / r 38 s 12

婦	woman / - / FU / # / r 38 s 11
婿	son in law; bridegroom / SEI / muko / r 38 s 12
婚	marriage / - / KON / # / r 38 s 10
娯	pleasure / - / GO / # / r 38 s 11

娠	pregnant / - / SHIN / # / r 38 s 10
姫	princess / - / # / hime / r 38 s 10
姻	marriage / - / IN / # / r 38 s 9

巧	skillful / - / KŌ / taku*mi* / r 48 s 5
功	merit; achievement / KŌ KU / # / r 19 s 5
攻	assault / - / KŌ / se*meru* / r 66 s 7
項	clause / - / KŌ / # / r 181 s 12
頂	summit; receive / CHŌ / itadaki itada+ / r 181 s 11

珠	pearl / - / SHU / # / r 96 s 10
球	ball / - / KYŪ / tama / r 96 s 11
現	present, visible, existing, actual / GEN / arawa*reru*.. / r 96 s 11
理	reasoning / - / RI / # / r 96 s 11

珍	rare; odd / CHIN / mezura*shii* / r 96 s 9
環	ring, circle / KAN / # / r 96 s 17
班	squad / - / HAN / # / r 96 s 10

1	33
2	34
3	35
4	36
5	37
6	38
7	39
8	40
9	41
10	42
11	43
12	44
13	45
14	46
15	47
16	48
17	49
18	50
19	51
20	52
21	53
22	54
23	55
24	56
25	57
26	58
27	59
28	60
29	61
30	62
31	63
32	64

■ 扣 抑 拓 抱 抛 拘

扣					
打 hit — DA *utsu* r64 s5	**払** pay; clear away FUTSU *harau* r64 s5	**扱** deal with — # *atsukau* r64 s6	**拝** pray; humble HAI *ogamu* r64 s8	**把** grasp HA # r64 s7	**押** push — Ō *osu..* r64 s8
抹 erase — MATSU # r64 s8	**扶** aid, support FU # r64 s7	**挟** sandwiched — KYŌ *hasamu..* r64 s9	**抄** excerpt — SHŌ # r64 s7	**拙** clumsy — SETSU # r64 s8	**推** infer; push, put forward SUI *osu* r64 s11
抽 draw out, extract CHŪ # r64 s8	**拍** clap; beat, tempo HAKU HYŌ # r64 s8	**捕** catch — HO *toru.. tsuka+* r64 s10			

抑					
挑 challenge — CHŌ *idomu* r64 s9	**排** repel, expel; anti- HAI # r64 s11	**批** critique — HI # r64 s7	**抑** restrain, suppress YOKU *osaeru* r64 s7	**推** infer; push, put forward SUI *osu* r64 s11	**掛** hang; cost; depend; … # *kakari ka+* r64 s11
搬 convey — HAN # r64 s13	**撤** withdraw — TETSU # r64 s15	**擬** imitate — GI # r64 s17			

拓					
拓 clear land — TAKU # r64 s8	**折** fold, snap; occasion SETSU *ori o+* r64 s7	**振** swing; shake SHIN *furuu..* r64 s10	**拡** expand — KAKU # r64 s8	**披** announce — HI # r64 s8	**抜** extract; omit; excel; … BATSU *nuku..* r64 s7
択 choose — TAKU # r64 s7	**据** install — # *sueru..* r64 s11	**掘** dig — KUTSU *horu* r64 s11	**握** grasp — AKU *nigiru* r64 s12		

拒 拠 拘			
拒 reject — KYO *kobamu* r64 s8	**拠** basis — KYO KO # r64 s8	**拘** arrest; cling to KŌ # r64 s8	**抱** embrace — HŌ *daku ida+ kaka+* r64 s8

8

技 skill - GI waza r64 s7	持 hold, have JI mo*tsu* r64 s9	拷 torture - GŌ # r64 s9	指 finger; point to SHI yubi sa+ r64 s9	捜 search SŌ saga*su* r64 s10	抗 oppose - KŌ # r64 s7
接 contact, touch SETSU tsu*gu* r64 s11	摘 pick, select TEKI tsu*mu* r64 s14	擁 hug; protect YŌ # r64 s16	擦 rub - SATSU su*reru.*. r64 s17	搾 squeeze - SAKU shibo*ru* r64 s13	控 hold back; wait; memo; ... KŌ hika*eru* r64 s11
描 depict - BYŌ ega*ku* r64 s11	措 set aside; dispose of SO # r64 s11	搭 embark - TŌ # r64 s12	撲 hit - BOKU # r64 s15	携 carry; take part KEI tazusa*eru.*. r64 s13	換 exchange - KAN kae*ru.*. r64 s12
抄 excerpt - SHŌ # r64 s7	拍 clap; beat, tempo HAKU HYŌ # r64 s8	捕 catch - HO to*ru.*. tsuka+ r64 s10			
拐 kidnap; deceive KAI # r64 s8	損 loss, harm; fail to SON soko*nau.*. r64 s13	操 fidelity; operate SŌ misao ayatsu+ r64 s16	投 throw; send in TŌ na*geru* r64 s7	招 invite - SHŌ mane*ku* r64 s8	掃 sweep - SŌ ha*ku* r64 s11
担 carry; take on TAN katsu*gu* nina+ r64 s8	提 proffer - TEI sa*geru* r64 s12	揚 raise; exalt; fried YŌ a*geru.*. r64 s12	掲 display; pin up KEI kaka*geru* r64 s11	撮 photograph - SATSU to*ru* r64 s15	摂 ingest; regent SETSU # r64 s13
括 fasten; lump together KATSU # r64 s9	挿 insert - SŌ sa*su* r64 s10	採 pick, gather, harvest SAI to*ru* r64 s11	授 confer; teach JU sazu*keru.*. r64 s11	援 aid - EN # r64 s12	揺 shake - YŌ yure*ru.*. r64 s12
抵 resist; a match for TEI # r64 s8	探 search - TAN sagu*ru* saga+ r64 s11	揮 wield; command KI # r64 s12	拾 pick up, acquire SHŪ JŪ hiro*u* r64 s9	捨 discard - SHA su*teru* r64 s11	

1	33
2	34
3	35
4	36
5	37
6	38
7	39
8	40
9	41
10	42
11	43
12	44
13	45
14	46
15	47
16	48
17	49
18	50
19	51
20	52
21	53
22	54
23	55
24	56
25	57
26	58
27	59
28	60
29	61
30	62
31	63
32	64

札 chit, tag, banknote SATSU fuda r 75 s 5	朴 simple - BOKU # r 75 s 6	材 timber; raw material ZAI # r 75 s 7	村 village - SON mura r 75 s 7	林 woods - RIN hayashi r 75 s 8	株 stocks, shares; stump # kabu r 75 s 10
棟 building; roof ridge TŌ mune muna- r 75 s 12	枚 sheet (of paper) MAI # r 75 s 8	桟 plank; jetty; bridge SAN # r 75 s 10	杉 Japanese cedar # sugi r 75 s 7	権 authority - KEN GON # r 75 s 15	
朽 decay - KYŪ kuchiru r 75 s 6	杯 cup, glass HAI sakazuki r 75 s 8	柄 handle; nature HEI gara e r 75 s 9	机 desk - KI tsukue r 75 s 6	相 mutual; minister SŌ SHŌ ai- r 109 s 9	根 root - KON ne r 75 s 10
桃 peach - TŌ momo r 75 s 10	柳 willow - RYŪ yanagi r 75 s 9	棚 shelf - # tana r 75 s 12	概 in general; roughly GAI # r 75 s 14	樹 tree - JU # r 75 s 16	極 extremes - KYOKU GOKU kiwami.. r 75 s 12
析 analyze - SEKI # r 75 s 8	板 board - HAN BAN ita r 75 s 8	植 plant - SHOKU ueru.. r 75 s 12			
械 apparatus, machine KAI # r 75 s 11	機 machine; opportunity KI hata r 75 s 16				
枢 pivotal - SŪ # r 75 s 8	欄 railing; column (in newspaper) RAN # r 75 s 20				

柏

柱	核	校	枯	枝	枠
pillar	nucleus	school	wither	branch	frame
-	-	-	-	-	#
CHŪ	KAKU	KŌ	KO	SHI	
hashira	#	#	kareru..	eda	waku
r 75 s 9	r 75 s 10	r 75 s 10	r 75 s 9	r 75 s 8	r 75 s 8
植	棺	棒	桜	楼	桟
plant	coffin	rod	cherry (tree, blossom)	tower	plank; jetty; bridge
-	-	-	Ō	-	SAN
SHOKU	KAN	BŌ	sakura	RŌ	#
ueru..	#	#		#	
r 75 s 12	r 75 s 12	r 75 s 12	r 75 s 10	r 75 s 13	r 75 s 10
棋	横	構	槽	模	様
game of *go*, *shogi*	side	build; care about	tank, tub	imitate	way, manner; Mr, Mrs
KI	-	KŌ	SŌ	-	YŌ
#	Ō	kamaeru	#	MO BO	sama
	yoko			#	
r 75 s 12	r 75 s 15	r 75 s 14	r 75 s 15	r 75 s 14	r 75 s 14
杉	格	梅			
Japanese cedar	state, condition	*ume*, plum, apricot			
#	KAKU KŌ	BAI			
sugi	#	ume			
r 75 s 7	r 75 s 10	r 75 s 10			
杯	柄	標	極	橋	
cup, glass	handle; nature	sign	extremes	bridge	
HAI	HEI	-	-	-	
sakazuki	gara e	HYŌ	KYOKU GOKU	KYŌ	
r 75 s 8	r 75 s 9	#	kiwami..	hashi	
		r 75 s 15	r 75 s 12	r 75 s 16	
松	栓	検			
pine tree	stopper	examine			
SHŌ	-	-			
matsu	SEN	KEN			
	#	#			
r 75 s 8	r 75 s 10	r 75 s 12			

1	33
2	34
3	35
4	36
5	37
6	38
7	39
8	40
9	41
10	42
11	43
12	44
13	45
14	46
15	47
16	48
17	49
18	50
19	51
20	52
21	53
22	54
23	55
24	56
25	57
26	58
27	59
28	60
29	61
30	62
31	63
32	64

■ 禾 米 耒

禾

私	利	秋	秒	秘	科
I; private	profit, benefit, (loan) interest	fall (autumn)	second (unit of time)	secret	(academic) subject
-	-	-	-	-	-
SHI	RI	SHŪ	BYŌ	HI	KA
watakushi	ki*ku*	aki	#	hi*meru*	#
r 115 s 7	r 18 s 7	r 115 s 9	r 115 s 9	r 115 s 10	r 115 s 9

称	秩	稚	租	和	
name, title	order, system	childish; infant	tax, tribute, levy	harmony; Japan	
-	-	-	-		
SHŌ	CHITSU	CHI	SO	WA O	
#	#	#	#	nago*mu*.. yawa+	
r 115 s 10	r 115 s 10	r 115 s 13	r 115 s 10	r 30 s 8	

種	稲	穏	税	移	程
seed; type of	rice plant	calm	tax	move, transfer	extent
SHU	-	-	ZEI	I	TEI
tane	TŌ	ON	#	utsu*ru*..	hodo
r 115 s 14	ine ina-	oda*yaka*	r 115 s 12	r 115 s 11	r 115 s 12
	r 115 s 14	r 115 s 16			

稼	稿	積	穂	穫	釈
earnings	manuscript	accumulate	tip of; ear of grain	harvest	explain
-	-	-	SUI	KAKU	SHAKU
KA	KŌ	SEKI	ho	#	#
kase*gu*	#	tsu*mu*..	r 115 s 15	r 115 s 18	r 165 s 11
r 115 s 15	r 115 s 15	r 115 s 16			

米

料	粗	粘	粒	粋	粉
fee; materials	coarse	sticky	particle, grain of	pure, elegant	flour, powder
RYŌ	-	-	RYŪ	SUI	FUN
#	SO	NEN	tsubu	#	kona ko
r 68 s 10	ara*i*	neba*ru*	r 119 s 11	r 119 s 10	r 119 s 10
	r 119 s 11	r 119 s 11			

精	糧	粧	糖	釈	
spirit, essence	provisions	cosmetics	sugar	explain	
SEI SHŌ	RYŌ RŌ	-	-	-	
#	kate	SHŌ	TŌ	SHAKU	
r 119 s 14	r 119 s 18	#	#	#	
		r 119 s 12	r 119 s 16	r 165 s 11	

耒

耗	耕	栽
use up, wear out	plow	plant
MŌ KŌ	-	-
#	KŌ	SAI
r 127 s 10	tagaya*su*	#
	r 127 s 10	r 75 s 10

■ ◫	ネ	ネ	方	牛	矢

ネ

礼	祈	祉	社	祥	禅
etiquette	pray	welfare	company, firm; society; shrine	auspicious	Zen
-	-	-	SHA	-	-
REI RAI	KI	SHI	yashiro	SHŌ	ZEN
#	inoru	#	#	#	#
r 113 s 5	r 113 s 7	r 113 s 7	r 113 s 7	r 113 s 7	r 113 s 7

祝	視	祖	神	福	禍
celebrate	look at, watch	ancestor	god	blessing, good fortune	calamity
-	-	-	-	-	-
SHUKU SHŪ	SHI	SO	SHIN JIN	FUKU	KA
iwau	#	#	kami kan- kō	#	#
r 113 s 7	r 147 s 11	r 113 s 7	r 113 s 7	r 113 s 7	r 113 s 7

ネ

補	被	初			
compensate; replenish	undergo, -ee; wear, cover	first time			
HO	HI	-			
oginau	kōmoru	SHO			
r 145 s 12	r 145 s 0	hatsu- ui- haji+ -so+			
		r 18 s 7			

裕	裸	褐	複	襟	
abundant	naked	brown	compound; duplicate	collar, neck	
-	-	-	FUKU	KIN	
YŪ	RA	KATSU	#	eri	
#	hadaka	#			
r 145 s 12	r 145 s 13	r 145 s 13	r 145 s 14	r 145 s 18	

方

放	旅	施	旋	族	旗
set free; emit	travel	do; donate	rotation	family	flag
HŌ	-	SHI SE	-	-	-
hanatsu..	RYO	hodokusu	SEN	ZOKU	KI
r 66 s 8	tabi	r 70 s 9	#	#	hata
	r 70 s 10		r 70 s 11	r 70 s 11	r 70 s 14

加					
add; join in					
KA					
kuwaeru..					
r 19 s 5					

牛

牧	物	牲	特	犠	
pasture	thing	sacrifice	special	sacrifice	
-	-	-	-	-	
BOKU	BUTSU MOTSU	SEI	TOKU	GI	
maki	mono	#	#	#	
r 93 s 8	r 93 s 8	r 93 s 9	r 93 s 10	r 93 s 17	

矢

知	短	矯			
know	short	rectify			
-	-	-			
CHI	TAN	KYŌ			
shiru	mijikai	tameru			
r 111 s 8	r 111 s 12	r 111 s 17			

1	33
2	34
3	35
4	36
5	37
6	38
7	39
8	40
9	41
10	42
11	43
12	44
13	45
14	46
15	47
16	48
17	49
18	50
19	51
20	52
21	53
22	54
23	55
24	56
25	57
26	58
27	59
28	60
29	61
30	62
31	63
32	64

糸▮

糾 inquire; twist KYŪ # r 120 s 9	**紅** crimson KŌ KU kurenai beni r 120 s 9	**紀** era; chronicle KI # r 120 s 9	**約** pledge; approx. YAKU # r 120 s 9	**紙** paper SHI kami r 120 s 10	**級** grade, rank KYŪ # r 120 s 9
紺 dark blue - KON # r 120 s 11	**紳** gentleman - SHIN # r 120 s 11	**練** training - REN neru r 120 s 14	**純** pure - JUN # r 120 s 10	**納** pay; obtain; store; supply NŌ NA NA' NAN TŌ osameru.. r 120 s 10	
組 group, union SO kumi ku+ r 120 s 11	**細** thin, fine SAI hosoi.. koma+ r 120 s 11	**紋** family crest MON # r 120 s 10	**紡** spin (yarn) - BŌ tsumugu r 120 s 10	**幻** illusion - GEN maboroshi r 52 s 4	**幼** infant - YŌ osanai r 52 s 5

糸▮

維 fiber; upkeep I # r 120 s 14	**縦** vertical; selfish JŪ tate r 120 s 16	**郷** hometown; rural KYŌ GŌ # r 163 s 11

糸▮

編 knit, edit HEN amu r 120 s 15

糸▮

継 inherit - KEI tsugu r 120 s 13	**縫** sew - HŌ nuu r 120 s 16

糸▮

約 pledge; approx. YAKU # r 120 s 9	**繊** fine, slender; fiber SEN # r 120 s 17	**織** weave - SHIKI SHOKU oru r 120 s 18

糸▮

綱 rope; gist KŌ tsuna r 120 s 14	**網** net - MŌ ami r 120 s 14	**納** pay; obtain; store; supply NŌ NA NA' NAN TŌ osameru.. r 120 s 10

組

糸組

紡	紋	絞	統	締	縮
spin (yarn) - BŌ tsumu*gu* r 120 s 10	family crest MON # r 120 s 10	strangle - KŌ shibo*ru* shi+ r 120 s 12	unite; rule, govern TŌ su*beru* r 120 s 12	tight; tie up TEI shi*meru*.. r 120 s 15	shrink - SHUKU chiji*maru*.. r 120 s 17

結	続	緒	緯	績
tie, bind KETSU musu*bu* yu+ r 120 s 12	continue - ZOKU tsuzu*ku*.. r 120 s 13	beginning; clue; cord SHO CHO o r 120 s 14	horizontal - I # r 120 s 16	achievement - SEKI # r 120 s 17

綿	線	縛	繕
cotton - MEN wata r 120 s 14	line - SEN # r 120 s 15	tie, bind BAKU shiba*ru* r 120 s 16	repair - ZEN tsukuro*u* r 120 s 18

緑	縁	絹	縄	繰	編
green - RYOKU ROKU midori r 120 s 14	edge; relation EN fuchi r 120 s 15	silk - KEN kinu r 120 s 13	rope - JŌ nawa r 120 s 15	reel, wind; move along; … # ku*ru* r 120 s 19	knit, edit HEN a*mu* r 120 s 15

紹	経	終	絡	絶
introduce - SHŌ # r 120 s 11	pass through; economics; … KEI KYŌ he*ru* r 120 s 11	end - SHŪ o*waru*.. r 120 s 11	entwine; link RAKU kara*mu*.. r 120 s 12	discontinue; die out ZETSU tae*ru*.. r 120 s 12

緩	紛	総	給	絵
slack - KAN yuru*mu*.. r 120 s 15	confuse - FUN magi*reru*.. r 120 s 10	general; whole SŌ # r 120 s 14	supply, pay KYŪ # r 120 s 12	picture - E KAI # r 120 s 12

1	33
2	34
3	35
4	36
5	37
6	38
7	39
8	40
9	41
10	42
11	43
12	44
13	45
14	46
15	47
16	48
17	49
18	50
19	51
20	52
21	53
22	54
23	55
24	56
25	57
26	58
27	59
28	60
29	61
30	62
31	63
32	64

口　日

口

叫	吐	吹	味	咲	呼
shout	spit; vomit	blow	taste	bloom	call
-	TO	-	MI	#	KO
KYŌ	haku	SUI	aji aji+	saku	yobu
sakebu		fuku			
r 30 s 6	r 30 s 6	r 30 s 7	r 30 s 8	r 30 s 9	r 30 s 8

吸	唯	鳴	唱	喝	
suck, inhale	only, sole	(animal) cry, howl; sound	chant	shout	
KYŪ	YUI I	MEI	SHŌ	KATSU	
suu	#	naku..	tonaeru	#	
r 30 s 6	r 30 s 11	r 196 s 14	r 30 s 11	r 30 s 11	

吟	唆	喚	嘆	噴	
recite	incite	call	sigh, grief	erupt	
-	-	-	TAN	-	
GIN	SA	KAN	nageku..	FUN	
#	sosonokasu	#		fuku	
r 30 s 7	r 30 s 10	r 30 s 12	r 30 s 13	r 30 s 15	

嘱	嚇	喫	可	句	
entrust	threaten	eat, drink, smoke	possible; approve	phrase	
-	-	KITSU	KA	-	
SHOKU	KAKU	#	#	KU	
#	#			#	
r 30 s 15	r 30 s 17	r 30 s 12	r 30 s 5	r 30 s 5	

日

昨	明	映			
yesterday, past	bright; next	reflect, shine; movie			
SAKU	MYŌ MEI	EI			
#	aku.. aki+ aka+	utsusu.. ha+			
r 72 s 9	r 72 s 8	r 72 s 9			

時	晩	暗	暁	晴	暖
time; hour	evening, late	dark, hidden	daybreak	fine weather	warm
JI	BAN	AN	-	SEI	-
toki	#	kurai	GYŌ	hareru..	DAN
			akatsuki		atatakai..
r 72 s 10	r 72 s 12	r 72 s 13	r 72 s 12	r 72 s 12	r 72 s 13

昭	暇	曜	旬	的	
clear, bright	leisure	day of week	10 day period	target; -like	
SHŌ	-	YŌ	JUN SHUN	TEKI	
#	KA	#	#	mato	
	hima				
r 72 s 9	r 72 s 13	r 72 s 18	r 72 s 6	r 106 s 8	

■ ■ 田 目 貝

1	33
2	34
3	35
4	36
5	37
6	38
7	39
8	40
9	41
10	42
11	43
12	44
13	45
14	46
15	47
16	48
17	49
18	50
19	51
20	52
21	53
22	54
23	55
24	56
25	57
26	58
27	59
28	60
29	61
30	62
31	63
32	64

田 目 貝

町
town, part of town
-
CHŌ
machi
r 102 s 7

畔
shore
-
HAN
#
r 102 s 10

略
abbreviate
-
RYAKU
#
r 102 s 11

眼
eye
-
GAN GEN
manako
r 109 s 11

眠
sleep
-
MIN
nemuru..
r 109 s 10

睡
sleep
-
SUI
#
r 109 s 13

瞬
moment; blink
-
SHUN
matataku
r 109 s 18

眺
view, look at
-
CHŌ
nagameru
r 109 s 11

助
help
-
JO
suke tasu+
r 19 s 7

則
rule
-
SOKU
#
r 18 s 9

財
finance; property
-
ZAI SAI
#
r 154 s 10

敗
be defeated
-
HAI
yabureru
r 66 s 11

貯
store up
-
CHO
#
r 154 s 12

賠
compensate
-
BAI
#
r 154 s 15

賜
give, bestow
-
SHI
tamawaru
r 154 s 15

贈
gift
-
ZŌ SŌ
okuru
r 154 s 18

購
buy
-
KŌ
#
r 154 s 17

販
sell, trade
HAN
#
r 154 s 11

賄
bribe; pay for
WAI
makanau
r 154 s 13

賊
robber
-
ZOKU
#
r 154 s 13

賦
tax; payment
FU
#
r 154 s 15

期
term; expect
KI
#
r 130* s 12

欺
deceive, cheat
GI
azamuku
r 76 s 12

歹

列	殊	残	
row, line	special	remain; cruel	
RETSU	- SHU	ZAN	
# koto	koto	nokosu..	
r 18 s 6	r 78 s 10	r 78 s 10	

殉	殖	死	外
martyr	increase, multiply	death	outside; foreign
- JUN	- SHOKU	- SHI	GAI GE
#	fueru..	shinu..	soto hoka hazu+
r 78 s 10	r 78 s 12	r 78 s 6	r 36 s 5

石

砂	砕	硝	硫	破	
sand	pulverize	gunpowder; nitric-	sulfur	break, ruin	
SA SHA	- SAI	- SHŌ	- RYŪ	- HA	
suna	kudakeru..	#	#	yaburu..	
r 112 s 9	r 112 s 9	r 112 s 12	r 112 s 12	r 112 s 10	

研	硬				
hone, grind, polish	hard, firm				
KEN	KŌ				
togu	katai				
r 112 s 9	r 112 s 12				

砲	碑	礁	確	磁	礎
cannon	monument	reef	certainty	magnet; porcelain	cornerstone
- HŌ	- HI	- SHŌ	- KAKU	- JI	- SO
#	#	#	tashka..	#	ishizue
r 112 s 10	r 112 s 14	r 112 s 17	r 112 s 15	r 112 s 14	r 112 s 18

酉

配	酢	酌	酷	酪	酔
distribute	vinegar	serve wine	severe	dairy produce	drunk
- HAI	- SAKU	- SHAKU	- KOKU	- RAKU	- SUI
kubaru	su	#	#	#	you
r 164 s 10	r 164 s 12	r 164 s 10	r 164 s 14	r 164 s 13	r 164 s 11

酵	酸	醜	醸	酬	
ferment	acid	ugly	brew	reward	
- KŌ	- SAN	- SHŪ	- JŌ	- SHŪ	
#	sui	minikui	kamosu	#	
r 164 s 14	r 164 s 14	r 164 s 17	r 164 s 20	r 164 s 13	

足

距	践	跡	跳	路
distance	carry out, put into practice	vestige, trace, footprints	jump	road, way
-			-	
KYO	SEN	SEKI	CHŌ	RO
#	#	ato	tobu ha+	-ji
r 157 s 12	r 157 s 13	r 157 s 13	r 157 s 13	r 157 s 13

踏	踊	躍
tread, stand on	dance	leap
TŌ	-	-
fumu..	YŌ	YAKU
	odoru..	odoru
r 157 s 15	r 157 s 14	r 157 s 21

虫

蚊	蛇
mosquito	snake
-	-
#	JA DA
ka	hebi
r 142 s 10	r 142 s 11

車

軒	転	軟	軌	軸
eaves	revolve; overturn	soft	track, orbit	axle, axis
-	TEN	-	KI	JIKU
KEN	korobu..	NAN	#	#
noki		yawaraka..		
r 159 s 10	r 159 s 11	r 159 s 11	r 159 s 9	r 159 s 12

軽	較	轄	輪	輸	載
light, slight	compare	jurisdiction, control	wheel, ring	transport	load; publish
KEI	-	KATSU	RIN	-	SAI
karui karo+	KAKU	#	wa	YU	noru..
	#			#	
r 159 s 12	r 159 s 13	r 159 s 17	r 159 s 15	r 159 s 16	r 159 s 13

卓

朝	乾	幹
morning; dynasty	dry	trunk, main part
CHŌ	-	KAN
asa	KAN	miki
	kawaku..	
r 130* s 12	r 5 s 11	r 51 s 13

耳

取	恥	聴	職	敢
take	shame; shy	listen	employment	daring
-	CHI	-	-	KAN
SHU	haji ha+	CHŌ	SHOKU	#
toru		kiku	#	
r 29 s 8	r 61 s 10	r 128 s 17	r 128 s 18	r 66 s 12

牙

邪	雅	刑	形
wicked	elegant	punishment	shape
-	-	-	-
JA	GA	KEI	KEI GYŌ
#	#	#	katachi kata
r 163 s 8	r 172 s 13	r 18 s 6	r 59 s 7

計 compute; plan — KEI — hakaru.. — r 149 s 9

討 attack — TŌ — utsu — r 149 s 10

記 write down — KI — shirusu — r 149 s 10

訳 translate — YAKU — wake — r 149 s 11

訂 revise — TEI — # — r 149 s 9

託 entrust — TAKU — # — r 149 s 10

許 permit — KYO — yurusu — r 149 s 11

詐 deceive — SA — # — r 149 s 12

証 proof, evidence — SHŌ — # — r 149 s 12

訪 visit — HŌ — tazuneru otozu+ — r 149 s 11

詠 recite or write poetry — EI — yomu — r 149 s 12

該 aforesaid; applicable — GAI — # — r 149 s 13

評 appraise — HYŌ — # — r 149 s 12

詳 detailed — SHŌ — kuwashii — r 149 s 13

訓 instruct — KUN — # — r 149 s 10

謝 thank; apology — SHA — ayamaru — r 149 s 17

訴 sue; appeal — SO — uttaeru — r 149 s 12

誕 birth — TAN — # — r 149 s 15

討 attack — TŌ — utsu — r 149 s 10

詞 word — SHI — # — r 149 s 12

試 try — SHI — tamesu kokoro+ — r 149 s 13

誠 sincerity — SEI — makoto — r 149 s 13

識 discern — SHIKI — # — r 149 s 19

誠 sincerity — SEI — makoto — r 149 s 13

調 tone; tune; inspect — CHŌ — shiraberu totono+ — r 149 s 15

詰	請	詩	誌	読
cram; rebuke	request	poem	magazine, journal	read
KITSU	- SEI SHIN	- SHI	- SHI	- DOKU TOKU TŌ
tsumu..	kou u+	#	#	yomu
r 149 s 13	r 149 s 15	r 149 s 13	r 149 s 14	r 149 s 14

訪	該	諸	誇	談	譲
visit	aforesaid; applicable	various	boast	talk	concede
- HŌ	- GAI	- SHO	- KO	- DAN	- JŌ
tazuneru otozu+	#	#	hokoru	#	yuzuru
r 149 s 11	r 149 s 13	r 149 s 15	r 149 s 13	r 149 s 15	r 149 s 20

諾	謹	護	謀	講
consent	respectful	protect	conspire	lecture
- DAKU	- KIN	- GO	- BŌ MU	- KŌ
#	tsutsushimu	#	hakaru	#
r 149 s 15	r 149 s 17	r 149 s 20	r 149 s 16	r 149 s 17

詠	詳	説	譜	謙	議
recite or write poetry	detailed	explanation	written record	modest	debate
EI	- SHŌ	- SETSU ZEI	FU	- KEN	- GI
yomu	kuwashii	toku	#	#	#
r 149 s 12	r 149 s 13	r 149 s 14	r 149 s 19	r 149 s 17	r 149 s 20

誤	謁	課	設	語
mistake	audience with	section; lesson	establish	language, word; talk
- GO	- ETSU	KA	- SETSU	GO
ayamaru	#	#	mōkeru	kataru..
r 149 s 14	r 149 s 15	r 149 s 15	r 149 s 11	r 149 s 14

詔	認	託	話	誘	謡
imperial edict	recognize	entrust	speak; tale	entice	song, chant
SHŌ	- NIN	- TAKU	WA	- YŪ	YŌ
mikotonori	mitomeru	#	hanashi hana+	sasou	utau
r 149 s 12	r 149 s 14	r 149 s 10	r 149 s 13	r 149 s 14	r 149 s 16

訟	診	論	諭
sue, accuse	diagnose	theory	admonish
SHŌ	- SHIN	- RON	- YU
#	miru	#	satosu
r 149 s 11	r 149 s 12	r 149 s 15	r 149 s 16

諮
consult
- SHI
hakaru
r 149 s 16

1	33		
2	34		
3	35		
4	36		
5	37		
6	38		
7	39		
8	40		
9	41		
10	42		
11	43		
12	44		
13	45		
14	46		
15	47		
16	48		
17	49		
18	50		
19	51		
20	52		
21	53		
22	54		
23	55		
24	56		
25	57		
26	58		
27	59		
28	60		
29	61		
30	62		
31	63		
32	64		

■◻ 月 舟

月

肌	肝	肺	肪	豚	肥
skin	liver	lungs	animal fat	pig	fatten, enrich
-	-	-	BŌ	-	HI
#	KAN	HAI	#	TON	koe ko+
hada	kimo	#		buta	
r 130 s 6	r 130 s 7	r 130 s 9	r 130 s 8	r 152 s 11	r 130 s 8

肢	脂	胎	腹	膜	腕
limb	animal fat	womb	abdomen	membrane	arm; skill
-	SHI	-	-	-	WAN
#	abura	TAI	FUKU	MAKU	ude
SHI		#	hara	#	
r 130 s 8	r 130 s 10	r 130 s 9	r 130 s 13	r 130 s 14	r 130 s 12

脱	朕	脳
remove; escape	I (imperial)	brain
DATSU	CHIN	NŌ
nugu..	#	#
r 130 s 11	r 130* s 10	r 130 s 11

勝	謄	騰	臓
victory; surpass	copy	(price) rise	entrails
SHŌ	-	-	ZŌ
katsu masa+	TŌ	TŌ	#
	#	#	
r 19 s 12	r 149 s 17	r 187 s 20	r 130 s 19

服	腸	腰	胆	脹
clothes; obey	intestine	loins, hips	gall bladder	expand
FUKU	-	YŌ	TAN	-
#	CHŌ	koshi	#	CHŌ
	#			#
r 130* s 8	r 130 s 13	r 130 s 13	r 130 s 9	r 130 s 12

脈	胴	胞	胸	脚	膨
vein, pulse	torso	placenta	bosom	leg, foot	swell
MYAKU	-	-	-	KYAKU KYA	-
#	DŌ	HŌ	KYŌ	ashi	BŌ
	#	#	mune muna-		fukureru..
r 130 s 10	r 130 s 10	r 130 s 9	r 130 s 10	r 130 s 11	r 130 s 16

舟

舶	航	般	船	艇	艦
large ship	navigate	sort, kind; time	ship	boat	warship
-	-	-	-	-	-
HAKU	KŌ	HAN	SEN	TEI	KAN
#	#	#	fune funa-	#	#
r 137 s 11	r 137 s 10	r 137 s 10	r 137 s 11	r 137 s 13	r 137 s 21

阝

阻	限	隅	陣	陳	防
obstruct	limit	corner	camp; formation	exhibit, declare	prevent
-	-	-	JIN	CHIN	BŌ
SO	GEN	GŪ	#	#	fusegu
habamu	kagiru	sumi			
r 170 s 8	r 170 s 9	r 170 s 12	r 170 s 10	r 170 s 11	r 170 s 7

陪	院	陸	陵	障
attend on	institute	land	imperial tomb	obstacle
-	-	-	RYŌ	-
BAI	IN	RIKU	misasagi	SHŌ
#	#	#		sawaru
r 170 s 11	r 170 s 10	r 170 s 11	r 170 s 11	r 170 s 14

隊	隣
crew, gang	neighbor
TAI	-
#	RIN
	tonari tona+
r 170 s 12	r 170 s 16

陽	隔	隠	陥	降	隆
sun; positive	apart; alternate, every other	conceal	collapse, cave in; trap	descend	prosper; high
YŌ	KAKU	-	KAN	KŌ	RYŪ
#	hedateru..	IN	ochiiru otoshii+	oriru.. fu+	#
		kakureru..			
r 170 s 12	r 170 s 13	r 170 s 14	r 170 s 10	r 170 s 10	r 170 s 11

除	険	陰	陛	階	際
remove	steep; risk	shade; negative	Your Majesty	floor, story; stairs; rank	occasion; edge
-	KEN	IN	HEI	KAI	SAI
JO JI	kewashii	kage kage+	#	#	kiwa
nozoku					
r 170 s 10	r 170 s 11	r 170 s 11	r 170 s 10	r 170 s 12	r 170 s 14

附	随	陶
attach	follow	pottery
-	-	-
FU	ZUI	TŌ
#	#	#
r 170 s 8	r 170 s 12	r 170 s 11

艮

即	既	門
Immediate; namely; i.e.	already	gate, door
SOKU	-	MON
#	KI	kado
	sude	
r 26 s 7	r 71* s 10	r 169 s 8

良

郎	朗	帥	師
man	cheerful; bright, clear	commander	teacher; army
-	-	-	SHI
RŌ	RŌ	SUI	#
#	hogaraka	#	
r 163 s 9	r 130* s 10	r 50 s 9	r 50 s 10

1	33
2	34
3	35
4	36
5	37
6	38
7	39
8	40
9	41
10	42
11	43
12	44
13	45
14	46
15	47
16	48
17	49
18	50
19	51
20	52
21	53
22	54
23	55
24	56
25	57
26	58
27	59
28	60
29	61
30	62
31	63
32	64

■ 金 食

金

針	鉢	鈍	鉄	銑	銃
needle	bowl, pot	dull, slow	iron	pig iron	gun
-	HACHI HATSU	DON	-	-	-
SHIN	#	DON	TETSU	SEN	JŪ
hari		nibui	#	#	#
r 167 s 10	r 167 s 13	r 167 s 12	r 167 s 13	r 167 s 14	r 167 s 14

錬	銀	錘	銭	鋳	録
refine; training	silver	spindle	coin	cast metal	record
REN	GIN	SUI	SEN	CHŪ	ROKU
#	#	omori tsumu	zeni	iru	#
r 167 s 16	r 167 s 14	r 167 s 16	r 167 s 14	r 167 s 15	r 167 s 16

錠	銑	鏡	鐘	鎮	錯
lock; pill	pig iron	mirror	bell	suppress	confused
JŌ	SEN	KYŌ	SHŌ	CHIN	SAKU
#	#	kagami	kane	shizumeru..	#
r 167 s 16	r 167 s 14	r 167 s 19	r 167 s 20	r 167 s 18	r 167 s 16

銘	鉛	鈴	鋭	鎖	
inscription	lead (the metal)	bell	sharp	chain; lock up	
-	EN	REI RIN	EI	SA	
MEI	namari	suzu	surudoi	kusari	
#					
r 167 s 14	r 167 s 13	r 167 s 13	r 167 s 15	r 167 s 18	

鉱	釣	銅	鋼	鍛	鑑
ore, mine	fishing; hanging	copper	steel	forge metal; training	model; take heed
KŌ	CHŌ	DŌ	KŌ	TAN	KAN
#	tsuru	#	hagane	kitaeru	#
r 167 s 13	r 167 s 11	r 167 s 14	r 167 s 16	r 167 s 17	r 167 s 23

食

飢	飯	飲	飾	館
hunger, starve	meal, cooked rice	drink	decorate	public building
KI	HAN	IN	-	KAN
ueru	meshi	nomu	SHOKU	#
r 184 s 10	r 184 s 12	r 184 s 12	kazaru	r 184 s 16
			r 184 s 13	

飼	飽	餓
raise, breed	sated	starve
SHI	-	-
kau	HŌ	GA
	akiru..	#
r 184 s 13	r 184 s 13	r 184 s 15

欧	殴		
Europe	assault		
-	-		
Ō	Ō		
#	nagu*ru*		
r 76 s 8	r 79 s 8		

駅	駐	駄	駆
station	reside, stay	no good, poor quality	spur on; drive; expel
-			
EKI	CHŪ	DA	KU
#	#	#	ka*ru..*
r 187 s 14	r 187 s 15	r 187 s 14	r 187 s 14

騎	験	騒	
ride a horse	examine; effect	noise, clamor	
KI	KEN GEN	SŌ	
#	#	sawa*gu*	
r 187 s 18	r 187 s 18	r 187 s 18	

勧	歓	観	
advise; encourage	delight	view; observe	
KAN	- KAN	KAN	
susu*meru*	#	#	
r 19 s 13	r 76 s 15	r 147 s 18	

鯨	鮮	触	解
whale	fresh, vivid	touch	unravel; solve
-	-	-	
GEI	SEN	SHOKU	KAI GE
kujira	aza*yaka*	sawa *fu+*	to*ku..*
r 195 s 19	r 195 s 17	r 148 s 13	r 148 s 13

◧

文 立 交 亥

対	効	郊	端	劾
oppose; pair	effective	outskirts, suburbs	edge; end; beginning; …	denounce, impeach
TAI TSUI	- KŌ	KŌ	TAN	GAI
#	kiku	#	hashi hata ha	#
r 41 s 7	r 19 s 8	r 163 s 9	r 117 s 14	r 19 s 8

由 京

畝	就	郭
ridge	start to	enclosure
se	- SHŪ JU	KAKU
#	tsuku..	#
une se	r 43 s 12	r 163 s 11
r 102 s 10		

古 青

故	静
old; dead; intent	quiet
KO	- SEI JŌ
yue	shizu shizu+
r 66 s 9	r 174 s 14

束 半 求 类

勅	頼	判	救	類
imperial edict	rely on; request	judge	rescue	sort, kind
CHOKU	RAI	- HAN BAN	- KYŪ	RUI
#	tayoru tano+	#	sukuu	#
r 19 s 9	r 181* s 16	r 18 s 7	r 66 s 11	r 181 s 18

音 音 竟

剖	部	韻	競
dissect	section	rhyme, tone	compete
- BŌ	- BU	IN	- KYŌ KEI
#	#	#	kisou se+
r 18 s 10	r 163 s 11	r 180 s 19	r 117 s 20

亲 彦 离 客

親	新	顔	離	額
parent, kin; intimate	new	face	separation	sum; frame; forehead
SHIN	SHIN	- GAN	- RI	GAKU
oya shita+	nii- atara+ ara+	kao	hanareru..	hitai
r 147 s 16	r 69 s 13	r 181 s 18	r 172 s 18	r 181 s 18

去 赤 圭 幸

却	赦	封	報	執
reject; exclude	pardon, forgive	seal up	report; reward	grasp; carry out
KYAKU	SHA	- FŪ HŌ	HŌ	SHITSU SHŪ
#	#	#	mukuiru	toru
r 26 s 7	r 155 s 11	r 41 s 9	r 32 s 12	r 32 s 11

寿 壹 壳 㝵

款	隷	鼓	殻	穀
clause; cordial	servant, subordinate	drum	shell	grain, cereal
KAN	REI	- KO	- KAKU	KOKU
#	#	tsuzumi	kara	#
r 76 s 12	r 171 s 16	r 207 s 13	r 79 s 11	r 115 s 14

■◻

七 上 ⺕

未 歩 歯

其 莫

片 川 厷

⺕ 丰 夬

朵 㬍

自

并 光 単

以	切	比	北
by means of; datum	cut	compare	north
I	-	HI	HOKU
#	SETSU SAI	kura*beru*	kita
r 9 s 5	ki*ru..*	r 81 s 4	r 21 s 5
	r 18 s 4		

叔	雌	頻	齢
aunt, uncle	female	frequent	age
SHUKU	SHI	HIN	REI
#	mesu me	#	#
r 29 s 8	r 172 s 14	r 181 s 17	r 211 s 17

収	欺	期	難
obtain; seize; collect; …	deceive, cheat	term; expect	difficult
SHŪ	GI	KI	NAN
osa*meru..*	azamu*ku*	#	kata*i muzuka+*
r 29* s 5	r 76 s 12	r 130* s 12	r 172 s 18

加	版	順	雄
add; join in	printing	sequence; obey	male; brave
KA	HAN	JUN	YŪ
kuwa*eru..*	#	#	osu o
r 19 s 5	r 91 s 8	r 181 s 12	r 172 s 12

兆	非	邦	規
sign, omen; trillion	un-, non-	homeland; Japan	regulation
CHŌ	HI	HŌ	KI
kiza*shi..*	#	#	#
r 10 s 6	r 175 s 8	r 163 s 7	r 147 s 11

郷	雑	能	
hometown; rural	miscellany	ability; *Noh* play	
KYŌ GŌ	ZATSU ZŌ	NŌ	
#	#	#	
r 163 s 11	r 172 s 14	r 130 s 10	

的	帥	師	
target; -like	commander	teacher; army	
TEKI	SUI	SHI	
mato	#	#	
r 106 s 8	r 50 s 9	r 50 s 10	

射	瓶	輝	戦
shoot	bottle	shine	war
SHA	BIN	KI	SEN
i*ru*	#	kayaga*ku*	ikusa tataka+
r 41 s 10	r 98 s 11	r 159 s 15	r 62 s 13

亻 釒 夂 夕	竹 bamboo - CHIKU take r 118 s 6	卸 wholesale - # oroshi oro+ r 26 s 9	処 deal with - SHO # r 16* s 5	外 outside; foreign GAI GE soto hoka hazu+ r 36 s 5
免 角	勉 diligent; strive BEN # r 19 s 10	触 touch - SHOKU sawa+ fu+ r 148 s 13	解 unravel; solve KAI GE toku.. r 148 s 13	
云 元 戸	魂 soul - KON tamashii r 194 s 14	頑 stubborn - GAN # r 181 s 13	所 place, site SHO tokoro r 63 s 8	
豆 鬲 雇	頭 head; top TŌ ZU TO atama kashira r 181 s 16	融 melt, fuse; dissolve YŪ # r 142 s 16	顧 look back - KO kaerimiru r 181 s 21	
丁 干 正 而	頂 summit; receive CHŌ itadaki itada+ r 181 s 11	刊 publish - KAN # r 18 s 5	政 government - SEI SHŌ matsurigoto r 66 s 9	耐 withstand - TAI taeru r 126 s 9
耳 开	敢 daring - KAN # r 66 s 12	刑 punishment - KEI # r 18 s 6	形 shape - KEI GYŌ katachi kata r 59 s 7	邪 wicked - JA # r 163 s 8 · 雅 elegant - GA # r 172 s 13
且 㬎 卩	助 help - JO suke tasu+ r 19 s 7	顕 obvious - KEN # r 181 s 18	門 gate, door - MON kado r 169 s 8	即 immediate; namely; i.e. SOKU # r 26 s 7 · 既 already - KI sude r 71 s 10
里 骨 咼	野 field; wild YA no r 166 s 11	髄 (bone) marrow ZUI # r 188 s 19	嗣 heir - SHI # r 30 s 13	

臨 attend; face RIN nozomu r 131 s 18	願 wish, request GAN negau r 181 s 19	殿 Mr, Mrs; palace DEN TEN tono -dono r 79 s 13

改 reform - KAI aratameru.. r 66 s 7	羽 feather, wing U ha hane r 124 s 6	弱 weak - JAKU yowai.. r 57 s 10	群 group - GUN mure.. mura r 123 s 13	郡 county, district GUN # r 163 s 10
双 pair; twin - SŌ futa r 29* s 4	預 deposit, entrust YO azukeru.. r 181 s 13	務 duties - MU tsutomeru.. r 19 s 11	疎 shun; sparse SO utomu.. r 103 s 12	
印 imprint, stamp; sign; India IN shirushi r 26 s 6	段 steps; rank DAN # r 79 s 9	卵 egg - RAN tamago r 26 s 7	邸 mansion - TEI # r 163 s 8	
乱 disorder - RAN midasu.. r 5 s 7	辞 word; resign JI yameru r 160 s 13	鶏 chicken - KEI niwatori r 196 s 19	釈 explain - SHAKU # r 165 s 11	彩 color - SAI irodoru r 59 s 11
領 territory - RYŌ # r 181 s 14	舗 shop; pavement HO # r 9* s 15	叙 describe - JO # r 29* s 9	頒 distribute - HAN # r 181 s 13	
刈 reap, mow # kaku r 18 s 4	疑 doubt - GI utagau r 103 s 14	殺 kill SATSU SETSU SAI korosu r 79 s 10		

丶 乚 丿 彡

丶

小	心	必	少		
small	heart	inevitable	few		
-	-	-	-		
SHŌ	SHIN	HITSU	SHŌ		
chiisai ko- o-	kokoro	kanarazu	sukoshi suku+		
r 42 s 3	r 61 s 4	r 61 s 5	r 42 s 4		
朴	外	掛	赴	以	似
simple	outside; foreign	hang; cost; depend; …	go to	by means of; datum	resemble
-	-	#	-	I	-
BOKU	GAI GE	kakari ka+	FU	#	JI
#	soto hoka hazu+		omomuku		niru
r 75 s 6	r 36 s 5	r 64 s 11	r 156 s 9	r 9 s 5	r 9 s 7
秒	抄	妙	砂	劣	省
second (unit of time)	excerpt	miraculous; odd	sand	inferior	minister; omit; reflect upon; …
BYŌ	-	-	-	-	-
#	SHŌ	MYŌ	SA SHA	RETSU	SHŌ SEI
	#	#	suna	otoru	habuku kaeri+
r 115 s 9	r 64 s 7	r 38 s 7	r 112 s 9	r 19 s 6	r 109 s 9
恥	泌	秘	称	跡	嚇
shame; shy	secrete	secret	name, title	vestige, trace, footprints	threaten
CHI	HITSU HI	-	SHŌ	SEKI	KAKU
haji ha+	#	HI	#	ato	#
r 61 s 10	r 85 s 8	himeru	r 115 s 10	r 157 s 13	r 30 s 17
		r 115 s 10			

乚

八	入	孤	弧
eight	enter; put in, let in	solitary, orphan	arc, arch
-	-	-	-
HACHI	NYŪ	KO	KO
ya ya'+ ya+ yō	hairu i+	#	#
r 12 s 2	r 11 s 2	r 39 s 8	r 57 s 9

丿

並	火	秋
line up; ordinary	fire; Tuesday	fall (autumn)
HEI	KA	SHŪ
narabu.. nami	hi ho	aki
r 1* s 8	r 86 s 4	r 115 s 9

彡

形	杉	彩	彰	影
shape	Japanese cedar	color	extol, commend	shadow
-	-	-	SHŌ	-
KEI GYŌ	#	SAI	#	EI
katachi kata	sugi	irodoru		kage
r 59 s 7	r 75 s 7	r 59 s 11	r 59 s 14	r 59 s 15
彫	膨			
carve	swell			
-	-			
CHŌ	BŌ			
horu	fukureru..			
r 59 s 11	r 130 s 16			

水 water; Wednesday SUI mizu r 85 s 4	永 eternal - EI nagai r 85 s 5	氷 ice - HYŌ kōri kō- hi r 85 s 5	求 seek, request KYŪ motomeru r 85 s 7	球 ball - KYŪ tama r 96 s 11	承 consent; be told SHŌ uketamawaru r 64 s 8
朴 simple - BOKU # r 75 s 6	外 outside; foreign GAI GE soto hoka hazu+ r 36 s 5	掛 hang; cost; depend; … # kakari ka+ r 64 s 11	赴 go to - FU omomuku r 156 s 9		
非 un-, non- HI # r 175 s 8	俳 haiku; actor HAI # r 9 s 10	排 repel, expel; anti- HAI # r 64 s 11			
作 make - SAKU SA tsukuru r 9 s 7	昨 yesterday, past SAKU # r 72 s 9	詐 deceive - SA # r 149 s 12	酢 vinegar - SAKU su r 164 s 12		
孔 hole KŌ # r 39 s 4	札 chit, tag, banknote SATSU fuda r 75 s 5	礼 etiquette - REI RAI # r 113 s 5	乱 disorder - RAN midasu.. r 5 s 7	乳 milk; breast NYŪ chichi chi r 5 s 8	沈 sink (into) - CHIN shizumu.. r 85 s 7
化 transform - KA KE bakeru.. r 21 s 4	比 compare - HI kuraberu r 81 s 4	北 north - HOKU kita r 21 s 5	批 critique - HI # r 64 s 7	靴 shoes - KA kutsu r 177 s 13	
死 death - SHI shinu r 78 s 6	尼 nun - NI ama r 44 s 5	泥 mud - DEI doro r 85 s 8			
兆 sign, omen; trillion CHŌ kizashi.. r 10 s 6	挑 challenge - CHŌ idomu r 64 s 9	桃 peach - TŌ momo r 75 s 10	跳 jump - CHŌ tobu ha+ . r 157 s 13	眺 view, look at CHŌ nagameru r 109 s 11	逃 escape - TŌ nigeru.. noga+ r 162 s 9

囗 丨 刂 少

丨

引	川	州	訓	酬	粛
pull	river	state, province; sandbank	instruct	reward	solemn; purge
-	-		-	-	
IN	SEN	SHŪ	KUN	SHŪ	SHUKU
hiku..	*kawa*	*su*	#	#	#
r 57 s 4	r 47 s 3	r 47 s 6	r 149 s 10	r 164 s 13	r 129 s 11

刂

刈	刊	刑	判	列	到
reap, mow	publish	punishment	judge	row, line	arrive
#	-	-	-	-	-
	KAN	KEI	HAN BAN	RETSU	TŌ
kaku	#	#	#	#	#
r 18 s 4	r 18 s 5	r 18 s 6	r 18 s 7	r 18 s 6	r 18 s 8
利	剰	刺	制	則	削
profit, benefit, (loan) interest	surplus	pierce	regulation	rule	whittle; reduce
	-		-		
RI	JŌ	SHI	SEI	SOKU	SAKU
kiku	#	*sasu..*	#	#	*kezuru*
r 18 s 7	r 18 s 11	r 18 s 8	r 18 s 8	r 18 s 9	r 18 s 9
刻	剤	剖	割	別	刷
carve; moment	medicine, drug	dissect	divide up	separate; other; special	print
		-	-		
KOKU	ZAI	BŌ	KATSU	BETSU	SATSU
kizamu	#	#	*wari wa+ sa+*	*wakareru*	*suru*
r 18 s 8	r 18 s 10	r 18 s 10	r 18 s 12	r 18 s 7	r 18 s 8
副	剣	創	剛	劇	
secondary, deputy	sword	create	strong	drama, dramatic	
	-	-	-		
FUKU	KEN	SŌ	GŌ	GEKI	
#	*tsurugi*	#	#	#	
r 18 s 11	r 18 s 10	r 18 s 12	r 18 s 10	r 18 s 15	
例	倒	側	測		
example	topple; inverted	side	measure		
-	-	-	-		
REI	TŌ	SOKU	SOKU		
tatoeru	*taoreru*	*kawa*	*hakaru*		
r 9 s 8	r 9 s 10	r 9 s 11	r 85 s 12		
痢	烈	愉			
diarrhea	intense	pleasure			
-	-	-			
RI	RETSU	YU			
#	#	#			
r 104 s 12	r 86 s 10	r 61 s 12			

少

抄	秒	妙	砂
excerpt	second (unit of time)	miraculous; odd	sand
-	-	-	-
SHŌ	BYŌ	MYŌ	SA SHA
#	#	#	*suna*
r 64 s 7	r 115 s 9	r 38 s 7	r 112 s 9

■　工　丁　亍　干　平

1	33
2	34
3	35
4	36
5	37
6	38
7	39
8	40
9	41
10	42
11	43
12	44
13	45
14	46
15	47
16	48
17	49
18	50
19	51
20	52
21	53
22	54
23	55
24	56
25	57
26	58
27	59
28	60
29	61
30	62
31	63
32	64

工

江 — inlet, river — KŌ — e — r 85 s 6
紅 — crimson — KŌ KU — kurenai beni — r 120 s 9
左 — left (hand) — SA — hidari — r 48 s 5
佐 — assistant — SA — # — r 9 s 7

丁

灯 — lamp — TŌ — hi — r 86 s 6
打 — hit — DA — utsu — r 64 s 5
訂 — revise — TEI — # — r 149 s 9
町 — town, part of town — CHŌ — machi — r 102 s 7
竹 — bamboo — CHIKU — take — r 118 s 6
寸 — tiny — SUN — # — r 41 s 3

可 — possible; approve — KA — # — r 30 s 5
河 — river — KA — kawa — r 85 s 8
何 — what, how many — KA — nani nan — r 9 s 7
伺 — visit; pay respects — SHI — ukagau — r 9 s 7
幻 — illusion — GEN — maboroshi — r 52 s 4

亍

行 — go; do; line — GYŌ KŌ AN — iku yu+ okona+ — r 144 s 6
術 — art, skill — JUTSU — # — r 60* s 11
街 — street, arcade — GAI KAI — machi — r 60* s 12
衝 — collide — SHŌ — # — r 60* s 15
衛 — guard — EI — # — r 60* s 16
衡 — balance, scales — KŌ — # — r 60* s 16

干

汗 — sweat — KAN — ase — r 85 s 6
肝 — liver — KAN — kimo — r 130 s 7
軒 — eaves — KEN — noki — r 159 s 10
許 — permit — KYO — yurusu — r 149 s 11

平

坪 — tsubo; floor area — # — tsubo — r 32 s 8
評 — appraise — HYŌ — # — r 149 s 12
呼 — call — KO — yobu — r 30 s 8

十 土 士 生 朱 失

十	汁 juice, soup JŪ shiru r 85 s 5	針 needle - SHIN hari r 167 s 10	計 compute; plan KEI haka*ru*.. r 149 s 9	

土	吐 spit; vomit TO ha*ku* r 30 s 6	社 company, firm; society; shrine SHA yashiro r 113 s 7	圧 pressure - ATSU # r 32 s 5	在 be located; exist; suburbs ZAI a*ru* r 32 s 6

士	仕 serve - SHI JI tsuka*eru* r 9 s 5	壮 grand, strong SŌ # r 32* s 6

生	性 sex; nature, essence SEI SHŌ # r 61 s 8	牲 sacrifice - SEI # r 93 s 9	姓 surname - SEI SHŌ # r 38 s 8

朱	株 stocks, shares; stump # kabu r 75 s 10	珠 pearl - SHU # r 96 s 10	殊 special - SHU koto r 78 s 10	味 taste - MI aji aji+ r 30 s 8	妹 younger sister MAI imōto r 38 s 8

失	秩 order, system CHITSU # r 115 s 10	鉄 iron - TETSU # r 167 s 13	銑 pig iron - SEN # r 167 s 14	洗 wash - SEN ara*u* r 85 s 9

弋 戈 戔

代 replace; era; price / DAI TAI / shiro ka+ yo / r 9 s 5
弐 two / - / NI / # / r 56* s 6
式 rite; style / SHIKI / # / r 154 s 15
武 military / BU MU / # / r 77 s 8
賦 tax; payment / FU / # / r 56 s 6
試 try / - / SHI / tamesu kokoro+ / r 149 s 13

伐 cut down / - / BATSU / # / r 9 s 6
戦 war / - / SEN / ikusa tataka+ / r 62 s 13
戯 play, frolic, jest / - / GI / tawamureru / r 62 s 15

我 I, my; self; selfish / GA / ware wa / r 62 s 7
戒 warn; command / - / KAI / imashimeru / r 62 s 7
械 apparatus, machine / - / KAI / # / r 75 s 11
栽 plant / - / SAI / # / r 75 s 10
裁 judge; cut / - / SAI / sabaku ta+ / r 145 s 12
載 load; publish / - / SAI / noru.. / r 159 s 13

域 area, zone / - / IKI / # / r 32 s 11
賊 robber / - / ZOKU / # / r 154 s 13
賦 tax; payment / FU / # / r 154 s 15
試 try / - / SHI / tamesu kokoro+ / r 149 s 13

繊 fine, slender; fiber / - / SEN / # / r 120 s 17
織 weave / - / SHIKI SHOKU / oru / r 120 s 18
職 employment / - / SHOKU / # / r 128 s 18
識 discern / - / SHIKI / # / r 149 s 19
餓 starve / - / GA / # / r 184 s 15
機 machine, opportunity / KI / hata / r 75 s 16

成 become; consist of / - / SEI JŌ / naru.. / r 62 s 6
威 power; threat / I / # / r 38 s 9
滅 perish; destroy / - / METSU / horobiru.. / r 85 s 13
減 decrease / - / GEN / heru / r 85 s 12
城 castle / - / JŌ / shiro / r 32 s 9
誠 sincerity / - / SEI / makoto / r 149 s 13

浅 shallow / - / SEN / asai / r 85 s 9
桟 plank; jetty; bridge / SAN / # / r 75 s 10
残 remain; cruel / - / ZAN / nokosu.. / r 78 s 10
践 carry out, put into practice / - / SEN / # / r 157 s 13
銭 coin / - / SEN / zeni / r 167 s 14

1	33
2	34
3	35
4	36
5	37
6	38
7	39
8	40
9	41
10	42
11	43
12	44
13	45
14	46
15	47
16	48
17	49
18	50
19	51
20	52
21	53
22	54
23	55
24	56
25	57
26	58
27	59
28	60
29	61
30	62
31	63
32	64

斗

料	斜	科
fee; materials	slant	(academic) subject
RYŌ	- SHA	KA
#	nana*me*	#
r 68　s 10	r 68　s 11	r 115　s 9

才

材	財
timber; raw material	finance; property
ZAI	ZAI SAI
#	#
r 75　s 7	r 154　s 10

寸

付	対	村	封	射	討
attach	oppose; pair	village	seal up	shoot	attack
- FU	TAI TSUI	- SON	FŪ HŌ	- SHA	- TŌ
tsu*ku..*	#	mura	#	i*ru*	u*tsu*
r 9　s 5	r 41　s 7	r 75　s 7	r 41　s 9	r 41　s 10	r 149　s 10

耐	尉	附	樹	謝	慰
withstand	military officer	attach	tree	thank; apology	console, cheer up
- TAI	I	- FU	- JU	SHA	I
ta*eru*	#	#	#	ayama*ru*	nagusa*meru*
r 126　s 9	r 41　s 11	r 170　s 8	r 75　s 16	r 149　s 17	r 61　s 15

犬

伏	状	獣	献	獄
prostrate; ambush	letter; state, condition	beast	offer gift	prison
FUKU	JŌ	- JŪ	- KEN KON	- GOKU
fu*u..*	#	kemono	#	#
r 9　s 6	r 94　s 7	r 94　s 16	r 94　s 13	r 94　s 14

就	駄
start to	no good, poor quality
- SHŪ JU	DA
tsu*ku..*	#
r 43　s 12	r 187　s 14

巾 甫 隹 主 羊

帥	師	布	怖
commander	teacher; army	cloth; spread	fear
-	SHI	FU	FU
SUI	#	nuno	kowai
#	r 50 s 10	r 50 s 5	r 61 s 8
r 50 s 9			

浦	捕	補	舗
bay; shore	catch	compensate; replenish	shop; pavement
HO	-	HO	HO
ura	HO	oginau	#
r 85 s 10	toru.. tsuka+	r 145 s 12	r 9* s 15
	r 64 s 10		

准	唯	推	稚	雅	維
quasi-; semi; ratify	only, sole	infer; push, put forward	childish; infant	elegant	fiber; upkeep
JUN	YUI I	SUI	CHI	GA	I
#	#	osu	#	#	#
r 15 s 10	r 30 s 11	r 64 s 11	r 115 s 13	r 172 s 13	r 120 s 14

雄	雑	雌	難	離
male; brave	miscellany	female	difficult	separation
YŪ	-	-	-	-
osu o	ZATSU ZŌ	SHI	NAN	RI
r 172 s 12	#	mesu me	katai muzuka+	hanareru..
	r 172 s 14	r 172 s 14	r 172 s 18	r 172 s 18

進	確
advance	certainty
-	-
SHIN	KAKU
susumu..	tashka..
r 162 s 11	r 112 s 15

注	住	往	柱	駐
pour; take note	dwell	go; bygone	pillar	reside, stay
CHŪ	-	Ō	-	CHŪ
sosogu	JŪ	#	CHŪ	#
r 85 s 8	sumu..	r 60 s 8	hashira	r 187 s 15
	r 9 s 7		r 75 s 9	

洋	祥	群	詳	鮮
ocean; Western	auspicious	group	detailed	fresh, vivid
YŌ	-	GUN	SHŌ	SEN
#	SHŌ	mure.. mura	kuwashii	azayaka
r 85 s 9	#	r 123 s 13	r 149 s 13	r 195 s 17
	r 113 s 7			

力 刀 勹

力

功	幼	助	効	劾	勅
merit; achievement	infant	help	effective	denounce, impeach	imperial edict
KŌ KU	- YŌ	- JO	- KŌ	- GAI	- CHOKU
#	osanai	suke tasu+	kiku	#	#
r 19 s 5	r 52 s 5	r 19 s 7	r 19 s 8	r 19 s 8	r 19 s 9

励	動	勤	勘	勧	働
encourage; diligent	move	work hard, serve	intuition; consider	advise; encourage	work
REI	- DŌ	KIN GON	KAN	KAN	- DŌ
hagemu..	ugoku..	tsutomeru	#	susumeru	hataraku
r 19 s 7	r 19 s 11	r 19 s 12	r 19 s 11	r 19 s 13	r 9 s 13

勉	協
diligent; strive	co-operate
BEN	- KYŌ
#	#
r 19 s 10	r 24 s 8

刀

切	初
cut	first time
- SETSU SAI	- SHO
kiru..	hatsu- ui- haji+ -so+
r 18 s 4	r 18 s 7

幻	辺	喫
illusion	vicinity	eat, drink, smoke
- GEN	- HEN	KITSU
maboroshi	atari -be	#
r 52 s 4	r 162 s 5	r 30 s 12

勹

的	酌	約	釣	均
target; -like	serve wine	pledge; approx.	fishing; hanging	equal
TEKI	- SHAKU	- YAKU	CHŌ	- KIN
mato	#	#	tsuru	#
r 106 s 8	r 164 s 10	r 120 s 9	r 167 s 11	r 32 s 7

立

文

交

亢

方

泣	位	粒
weep, cry	rank; approx.	particle, grain of
KYŪ	I	RYŪ
na*ku*	kurai	tsubu
r 85　s 8	r 9　s 7	r 119　s 11

蚊	紋
mosquito	family crest
-	MON
#	#
ka	
r 142　s 10	r 120　s 10

校	較	絞
school	compare	strangle
-	-	-
KŌ	KAKU	KŌ
#	#	shibo*ru* shi+
r 75　s 10	r 159　s 13	r 120　s 12

坑	抗	航
pit	oppose	navigate
-	-	-
KŌ	KŌ	KŌ
#	#	#
r 32　s 7	r 64　s 7	r 137　s 10

坊	妨	防	肪	紡
boy; priest	obstruct	prevent	animal fat	spin (yarn)
BŌ BO'	-	-	BŌ	BŌ
#	BŌ	BŌ	#	BŌ
	samata*geru*	fuse*gu*		tsumu*gu*
r 32　s 7	r 38　s 7	r 170　s 7	r 130　s 8	r 120　s 10

訪
visit
-
HŌ
tazu*neru* otozu+
r 149　s 11

欠

次	炊	吹	欧	軟	欺
next	cook, boil	blow	Europe	soft	deceive, cheat
JI SHI	SUI	SUI	Ō	NAN	GI
tsugi tsu+	ta*ku*	fu*ku*	#	yawa*raka*..	azamu*ku*
r 76 s 6	r 86 s 8	r 30 s 7	r 76 s 8	r 159 s 11	r 76 s 12

欲	飲	款	歓	歌	
desire	drink	clause; cordial	delight	song, sing	
YOKU	IN	KAN	KAN	KA	
hos*suru* ho+	no*mu*	#	#	uta uta+	
r 76 s 11	r 184 s 12	r 76 s 12	r 76 s 15	r 76 s 14	

畝	称				
ridge	name, title				
se	-				
#	SHŌ				
une se	#				
r 102 s 10	r 115 s 10				

攵

攻	改	枚	牧	政	放
assault	reform	sheet (of paper)	pasture	government	set free; emit
-	-	MAI	-	SEI SHŌ	HŌ
KŌ	KAI	#	BOKU	matsurigoto	hana*tsu*..
se*meru*	arata*meru*..		maki		
r 66 s 7	r 66 s 7	r 75 s 8	r 93 s 8	r 66 s 9	r 66 s 8

救	敗	敢	敏	故	致
rescue	be defeated	daring	agile, alert	old; dead; intent	cause; do
-	HAI	-	-	KO	CHI
KYŪ	yabu*reru*	KAN	BIN	yue	ita*su*
suku*u*		#	#		
r 66 s 11v	r 66 s 11	r 66 s 12	r 66 s 10	r 66 s 9	r 133 s 10

赦	教	散	敬		
pardon, forgive	teach	scatter	respect		
SHA	KYŌ	-	-		
#	oshi*eru* oso+	SAN	KEI		
		chi*ru*..	uyama*u*		
r 155 s 11	r 66 s 11	r 66 s 12	r 66 s 12		

数	敵	敷			
number	enemy	spread			
SŪ SU	TEKI	FU			
kazu kazo+	kataki	shi*ku*			
r 66 s 13	r 66 s 15	r 66 s 15			

倣	徴	微	徹	撤	激
imitate	symptom; levy	tiny, faint, hard to see	thorough	withdraw	violent
-	CHŌ	BI	-	TETSU	GEKI
HŌ	#	#	TETSU	#	hage*shii*
nara*u*			#		
r 9 s 10	r 60 s 14	r 60 s 13	r 60 s 15	r 64 s 15	r 85 s 16

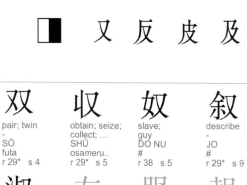

又 反 皮 及

又

双	収	奴	叙	取	叔
pair; twin	obtain; seize; collect; …	slave; guy	describe	take	aunt, uncle
-	SŌ futa	SHŪ osameru..	DO NU	JO	SHU toru
SŌ futa r 29* s 4	SHŪ osameru.. r 29* s 5	DO NU # r 38 s 5	JO # r 29* s 9	SHU toru r 29 s 8	SHUKU # r 29 s 8

淑	友	服	報	極	趣
graceful	friend	clothes; obey	report; reward	extremes	gist; motive; elegance
- SHUKU # r 85 s 11	- YŪ tomo r 29 s 4	FUKU # r 130* s 8	HŌ mukuiru r 32 s 12	- KYOKU GOKU kiwami.. r 75 s 12	SHU omomuki r 156 s 15

反

仮	坂	板	版	販	飯
temporary	slope	board	printing	sell, trade	meal, cooked rice
- KA KE kari r 9 s 6	- HAN saka r 32 s 7	- HAN BAN ita r 75 s 8	- HAN # r 91 s 8	HAN # r 154 s 11	HAN meshi r 184 s 12

返
return, repay
HEN.. kaeru.. r 162 s 7

皮

波	披	彼	破	被
waves	announce	he, she, they; that (yonder)	break, ruin	undergo, -ee; wear, cover
- HA nami r 85 s 8	- HI # r 64 s 8	HI kare kano r 60 s 8	- HA yaburu.. r 112 s 10	HI kōmoru r 145 s 0

及

吸	扱	級
suck, inhale	deal with	grade, rank
KYŪ suu r 30 s 6	- # atsukau r 64 s 6	KYŪ # r 120 s 9

1	33
2	34
3	35
4	36
5	37
6	38
7	39
8	40
9	41
10	42
11	43
12	44
13	45
14	46
15	47
16	48
17	49
18	50
19	51
20	52
21	53
22	54
23	55
24	56
25	57
26	58
27	59
28	60
29	61
30	62
31	63
32	64

己 包 也 屯

己				
妃	記	紀	配	起
queen, empress	write down	era; chronicle	distribute	wake up, rise; begin
HI	-	KI	-	KI
#	KI	#	HAI	okiru..
r 38 s 6	shirusu	r 120 s 9	kubaru	r 156 s 10
	r 149 s 10		r 164 s 10	

包				
泡	胞	砲	飽	抱
bubbles	placenta	cannon	sated	embrace
-	-	-	-	-
HŌ	HŌ	HŌ	HŌ	HŌ
awa	#	#	akiru..	daku ida+ kaka+
r 85 s 8	r 130 s 9	r 112 s 10	r 184 s 13	r 64 s 8

也			
池	他	地	
pond	other	earth, ground; place	
-	-	CHI JI	
CHI	TA	#	
ike	#	r 32 s 6	
r 85 s 6	r 9 s 5		

屯		
純	鈍	
pure	dull, slow	
-	DON	
JUN	nibui	
#	r 167 s 12	
r 120 s 10		

几 斤 旡

机 desk - KI tsukue r 75 s 6

肌 skin - # hada r 130 s 6

飢 hunger, starve KI ueru r 184 s 10

帆 sail - HAN ho r 50 s 6

処 deal with - SHO # r 16* s 5

拠 basis - KYO KO # r 64 s 8

折 fold, snap; occasion SETSU ori o+ r 64 s 7

析 analyze - SEKI # r 75 s 8

祈 pray - KI inoru r 113 s 7

所 place, site SHO tokoro r 63 s 8

新 new - SHIN nii- atara+ ara+ r 69 s 13

断 sever; decide DAN kotowaru ta+ r 69 s 11

漸 gradually - ZEN r 85 s 14

近 near; recent KIN chikai r 162 s 7

匠 craftsman - SHŌ # r 22 s 6

逝 die, death SEI yuku r 162 s 10

訴 sue; appeal SO uttaeru r 149 s 12

既 already - KI sude r 71 s 10

慨 deplore - GAI # r 61 s 13

概 in general; roughly GAI # r 75 s 14

■ 口 田 由 申 甲

口	**加** add; join in KA kuwa*eru*.. r 19　s 5	**如** as, like, such as JO NYO # r 38　s 6	**知** know - CHI shi*ru* r 111　s 8	**和** harmony; Japan WA O nago*mu*.. yawa+ r 30　s 8
田	**畑** field - # hata hatake r 102　s 9	**細** thin, fine SAI hoso*i*.. koma+ r 120　s 11		
由	**油** oil - YU abura r 85　s 8	**抽** draw out, extract CHŪ # r 64　s 8	**軸** axle, axis JIKU # r 159　s 12	
申	**伸** extend, stretch SHIN no*biru*.. r 9　s 7	**神** god - SHIN JIN kami kan- kō r 113　s 7	**紳** gentleman - SHIN # r 120　s 11	**沖** open sea - CHŪ oki r 85　s 7 ‖ **仲** relationship - CHŪ naka r 9　s 6
甲	**押** push - Ō o*su*.. r 64　s 8	**岬** headland, cape # misaki r 46　s 8		

白

且

見

頁

泊 overnight - HAKU to*maru*.. r 85 s 8	伯 aunt, uncle; earl HAKU # r 9 s 7	拍 clap; beat, tempo HAKU HYŌ # r 64 s 8	舶 large ship - HAKU # r 137 s 11	旧 old, former KYŪ # r 72* s 5

阻 obstruct - SO haba*mu* r 170 s 8	祖 ancestor - SO # r 113 s 7	租 tax, tribute, levy SO # r 115 s 10	粗 coarse - SO ara*i* r 119 s 11	組 group, union SO kumi ku+ r 120 s 11	相 mutual; minister SŌ SHŌ ai- r 109 s 9

規 regulation - KI # r 147 s 11	視 look at, watch SHI # r 147 s 11	現 present, visible, existing, actual GEN arawa*reru*.. r 96 s 11	親 parent, kin; intimate SHIN oya shita+ r 147 s 16	観 view; observe KAN # r 147 s 18

頂 summit; receive CHŌ itadaki itada+ r 181 s 11	項 clause - KŌ # r 181 s 12	煩 trouble, worry HAN BON wazura*u*.. r 86 s 13	頼 rely on; request RAI tayo*ru* tano+ r 181* s 16

頒 distribute - HAN # r 181 s 13	領 territory - RYŌ # r 181 s 14	額 sum; frame; forehead GAKU hitai r 181 s 18	頻 frequent - HIN # r 181 s 17	類 sort, kind RUI # r 181 s 18

頑 stubborn - GAN # r 181 s 13	預 deposit, entrust YO azuke*ru*.. r 181 s 13	頭 head; top TŌ ZU TO atama kashira r 181 s 16	顕 obvious - KEN # r 181 s 18

順 sequence; obey JUN # r 181 s 12	傾 inclination - KEI katamu*ku*.. r 9 s 13	瀬 shallows, rapids # se r 85 s 19

顔 face - GAN kao r 181 s 18	願 wish, request - GAN nega*u* r 181 s 19	顧 look back - KO kaeri*miru*.. r 181 s 21	題 title, topic DAI # r 181 s 18

1	33
2	34
3	35
4	36
5	37
6	38
7	39
8	40
9	41
10	42
11	43
12	44
13	45
14	46
15	47
16	48
17	49
18	50
19	51
20	52
21	53
22	54
23	55
24	56
25	57
26	58
27	59
28	60
29	61
30	62
31	63
32	64

卩

印	却	即	卸	犯	卵
imprint, stamp; sign; India	reject; exclude	immediate; namely; i.e.	wholesale	crime	egg
IN	KYAKU	SOKU	-	HAN	RAN
shirushi	#	#	oroshi oro+	okasu	tamago
r 26 s 6	r 26 s 7	r 26 s 7	r 26 s 9	r 94 s 5	r 26 s 7

仰	抑	柳	脚	御	迎
look up at; respect	restrain, suppress	willow	leg, foot	(honorific); control	welcome
GYŌ KŌ	YOKU	RYŪ	KYAKU KYA	GYO GO	GEI
aogu ō+	osaeru	yanagi	ashi	on-	mukaeru
r 9 s 6	r 64 s 7	r 75 s 9	r 130 s 11	r 60 s 12	r 162 s 7

阝

邦	邪	郡	郎	郊	邸
homeland; Japan	wicked	county, district	man	outskirts, suburbs	mansion
HŌ	JA	GUN	RŌ	KŌ	TEI
-	#	#	#	#	#
r 163 s 7	r 163 s 8	r 163 s 10	r 163 s 9	r 163 s 9	r 163 s 8

部	郭	都	郵	郷	廊
section	enclosure	city, capital	mail	hometown; rural	corridor
BU	KAKU	TO TSU	YŪ	KYŌ GŌ	RŌ
#	#	miyako	#	#	#
r 163 s 11	r 163 s 11	r 163 s 11	r 163 s 11	r 163 s 11	r 53 s 12

尺

沢	択	訳	釈	駅
marsh; plenty; ...	choose	translate	explain	station
TAKU	TAKU	YAKU	SHAKU	EKI
sawa	#	wake	#	#
r 85 s 7	r 64 s 7	r 149 s 11	r 165 s 11	r 187 s 14

月

明	朗	朝	期
bright; next	cheerful; bright, clear	morning; dynasty	term; expect
MYŌ MEI	RŌ	CHŌ	KI
aku.. aki+ aka+	hogaraka	asa	#
r 72 s 8	r 130* s 10	r 130* s 12	r 130* s 12

湖	潮	棚
lake	tide; seawater	shelf
KO	CHŌ	-
mizuumi	shio	#
r 85 s 12	r 85 s 15	tana
		r 75 s 12

有	賄	随	髄	門
have; exist	bribe; pay for	follow	(bone) marrow	gate, door
YŪ U	WAI	-	ZUI	MON
aru	makanau	ZUI	#	kado
r 130* s 6	r 154 s 13	#	r 188 s 19	r 169 s 8
		r 170 s 12		

艮

艮

良

司

服	報	眠		
clothes; obey	report; reward	sleep		
FUKU	HŌ	-		
#	mukuiru	MIN		
r 130* s 8	r 32 s 12	nemuru..		
		r 109 s 10		

恨	根	限	眼	銀
grudge; regret	root	limit	eye	silver
KON	KON	GEN	GAN GEN	GIN
uramu..	ne	kagiru	manako	#
r 61 s 9	r 75 s 10	r 170 s 9	r 109 s 11	r 167 s 14

退	眠
retreat	sleep
TAI	MIN
shirizoku..	nemuru..
r 162 s 9	r 109 s 10

浪	娘
waves; roam	daughter
RŌ	-
#	musume
r 85 s 10	r 38 s 10

伺	詞	飼	嗣
visit; pay respects	word	raise, breed	heir
SHI	SHI	SHI	SHI
ukagau	#	kau	#
r 9 s 7	r 149 s 12	r 184 s 13	r 30 s 13

1	33
2	34
3	35
4	36
5	37
6	38
7	39
8	40
9	41
10	42
11	43
12	44
13	45
14	46
15	47
16	48
17	49
18	50
19	51
20	52
21	53
22	54
23	55
24	56
25	57
26	58
27	59
28	60
29	61
30	62
31	63
32	64

ム 区 乍 長

ム	

仏
Buddha;
France
BUTSU
hotoke
r 9 s 4

払
pay;
clear away
FUTSU
hara*u*
r 64 s 5

私
I; private
-
SHI
watakushi
r 115 s 7

区

枢
pivotal
-
SŪ
#
r 75 s 8

駆
spur on;
drive; expel
KU
karu..
r 187 s 14

乍

作
make
-
SAKU SA
tsuku*ru*
r 9 s 7

昨
yesterday,
past
SAKU
#
r 72 s 9

酢
vinegar
-
SAKU
su
r 164 s 12

詐
deceive
-
SA
#
r 149 s 12

許
permit
-
KYO
yuru*su*
r 149 s 11

長

張
stretch
-
CHŌ
ha*ru*
r 57 s 11

帳
notebook;
curtain
CHŌ
#
r 50 s 11

脹
expand
-
CHŌ
ha*reru* fuku+
r 130 s 12

■ 虫 鳥 鬼

虫

鳥

鬼

独	触	融	沖	仲
alone; Germany	touch	melt, fuse; dissolve	open sea	relationship
DOKU	- SHOKU	YŪ	- CHŪ	- CHŪ
hito*ri*	sawa *fu*+	#	oki	naka
r 94 s 9	r 148 s 13	r 142 s 16	r 85 s 7	r 9 s 6

鳴	鶏
(animal) cry, howl; sound	chicken
MEI	- KEI
na*ku*..	niwatori
r 196 s 14	r 196 s 19

塊	魂	醜
lump	soul	ugly
- KAI	- KON	- SHŪ
katamari	tamashii	miniku*i*
r 32 s 13	r 194 s 14	r 164 s 17

1	33
2	34
3	35
4	36
5	37
6	38
7	39
8	40
9	41
10	42
11	43
12	44
13	45
14	46
15	47
16	48
17	49
18	50
19	51
20	52
21	53
22	54
23	55
24	56
25	57
26	58
27	59
28	60
29	61
30	62
31	63
32	64

■ 殳 攴 圣 卆

殳

没	役	投	殴	段	般
sink; die; disappear	service, duty	throw; send in	assault	steps; rank	sort, kind; time
BOTSU	EKI YAKU	TŌ	Ō	DAN	HAN
#	#	na*geru*	nagu*ru*	#	#
r 85 s 7	r 60 s 7	r 64 s 7	r 79 s 8	r 79 s 9	r 137 s 10

設	殻	穀	殺
establish	shell	grain, cereal	kill
-	-	-	-
SETSU	KAKU	KOKU	SATSU SETSU SAI
mō*keru*	kara	#	koro*su*
r 149 s 11	r 79 s 11	r 115 s 14	r 79 s 10

搬	鍛	殿
convey	forge metal; training	Mr, Mrs; palace
-		
HAN	TAN	DEN TEN
#	kita*eru*	tono -dono
r 64 s 13	r 167 s 17	r 79 s 13

攴

技	枝	岐	肢	鼓
skill	branch	diverge	limb	drum
	-		-	
GI	SHI	KI	SHI	KO
waza	eda	#	#	tsuzumi
r 64 s 7	r 75 s 8	r 46 s 7	r 130 s 8	r 207 s 13

圣

径	怪	軽	経
path; diameter	strange, weird, spooky	light, slight	pass through; economics; …
KEI	KAI	KEI	KEI KYŌ
#	aya*shii*..	karu*i* karo+	he*ru*
r 60 s 8	r 61 s 8	r 159 s 12	r 120 s 11

卆

枠	粋	砕	酔
frame	pure, elegant	pulverize	drunk
-	SUI	-	-
#	#	SAI	SUI
waku		kuda*keru*..	yo*u*
r 75 s 8	r 119 s 10	r 112 s 9	r 164 s 11

■ 分 令 僉 青 寺

分

粉	紛
flour, powder	confuse
FUN	-
kona ko	FUN
r 119 s 10	magi*reru*..
	r 120 s 10

令

鈴	齢	冷
bell	age	cold
-	-	-
REI RIN	REI	REI
suzu	#	tsume*tai* hi+ sa+
r 167 s 13	r 211 s 17	r 15 s 7

僉

倹	検	険	験
thrifty	examine	steep; risk	examine; effect
-	-	KEN	KEN GEN
KEN	KEN	kewa*shii*	#
#	#	r 170 s 11	r 187 s 18
r 9 s 10	r 75 s 12		

青

精	晴	請	清	漬	債
spirit, essence	fine weather	request	pure	pickle	debt
SEI SHŌ	SEI	-	SEI SHŌ	#	SAI
#	ha*reru*..	SEI SHIN	kiyo*i*..	tsu*keru*..	#
r 119 s 14	r 72 s 12	ko*u* u+	r 85 s 11	r 85 s 14	r 9 s 13
		r 149 s 15			

寺

侍	待	持	特	時	詩
samurai; serve	await	hold, have	special	time; hour	poem
JI	-	JI	-	JI	-
samurai	TAI	mo*tsu*	TOKU	toki	SHI
r 9 s 8	ma*tsu*	r 64 s 9	#	r 72 s 10	#
	r 60 s 9		r 93 s 10		r 149 s 13

■ 㕣 谷 台 各 舌

㕣					
沿 along - EN sou r 85 s 8	船 ship - SEN fune funa- r 137 s 11	鉛 lead (the metal) EN namari r 167 s 13			
谷					
浴 bathe - YOKU abiru.. r 85 s 10	俗 vulgar; custom - ZOKU # r 9 s 9	裕 abundant - YŪ # r 145 s 12	給 supply, pay KYŪ # r 120 s 12	拾 pick up, acquire SHŪ JU hirou r 64 s 9	捨 discard - SHA suteru r 64 s 11
台					
治 govern; heal JI CHI naoru.. osa+ r 85 s 8	始 begin - SHI hajimaru.. r 38 s 8	胎 womb - TAI # r 130 s 9			
各					
格 state, condition KAKU KŌ # r 75 s 10	略 abbreviate - RYAKU # r 102 s 11	路 road, way RO -ji r 157 s 13	酪 dairy produce RAKU # r 164 s 13	絡 entwine; link RAKU karamu.. r 120 s 12	銘 inscription - MEI # r 167 s 14
舌					
活 active - KATSU # r 85 s 9	括 fasten; lump together KATSU # r 64 s 9	話 speak; tale WA hanashi hana+ r 149 s 13	粘 sticky - NEN nebaru r 119 s 11		

■ 召 兑

沼	招	昭	詔	紹
marsh	invite	clear, bright	imperial edict	introduce
-	-	-	-	-
SHŌ	SHŌ	SHŌ	SHŌ	SHŌ
numa	mane*ku*	#	mikotonori	#
r 85 s 8	r 64 s 8	r 72 s 9	r 149 s 12	r 120 s 11

悦	税	脱	説	鋭
joy	tax	remove; escape	explanation	sharp
-	-	-	-	-
ETSU	ZEI	DATSU	SETSU ZEI	EI
#	#	nu*gu*..	to*ku*	surudo*i*
r 61 s 10	r 115 s 12	r 130 s 11	r 149 s 14	r 167 s 15

況	祝
conditions	celebrate
-	-
KYŌ	SHUKU SHŪ
#	iwa*u*
r 85 s 8	r 113 s 7

方 辛 京 竞

広 東 隷

止 本 未

占 中

先 告

关 半

㠯

丩 甘 井

訪	辞	涼	鯨	競
visit	word; resign	cool	whale	compete
-	JI	-	-	-
HŌ	yameru	RYŌ	GEI	KYŌ KEI
tazuneru otozu+		suzushii..	kujira	kisou se+
r 149 s 11	r 160 s 13	r 85 s 11	r 195 s 19	r 117 s 20

鉱	疎	隷		
ore, mine	shun; sparse	servant, subordinate		
KŌ	SO	REI		
#	utomu..	#		
r 167 s 13	r 103 s 12	r 171 s 16		

祉	鉢	味	妹	
welfare	bowl, pot	taste	younger sister	
-	HACHI HATSU	-	-	
SHI	#	MI	MAI	
#		aji aji+	imōto	
r 113 s 7	r 167 s 13	r 30 s 8	r 38 s 8	

粘	仲	沖		
sticky	relationship	open sea		
-	-	-		
NEN	CHŪ	CHŪ		
nebaru	naka	oki		
r 119 s 11	r 9 s 6	r 85 s 7		

洗	銑	酷		
wash	pig iron	severe		
-	-	-		
SEN	SEN	KOKU		
arau	#	#		
r 85 s 9	r 167 s 14	r 164 s 14		

咲	朕	畔		
bloom	I, we (imperial)	shore		
-	CHIN	HAN		
#	#	#		
saku				
r 30 s 9	r 74 s 10	r 102 s 10		

能				
ability; Noh play				
NŌ				
#				
r 130 s 10				

叫	紺	耕	併	
shout	dark blue	plow	combine, unite	
-	-	-	HEI	
KYŌ	KON	KŌ	awaseru	
sakebu	#	tagayasu		
r 30 s 6	r 120 s 11	r 127 s 10	r 9 s 8	

人 太 火

九 丸 尤 内

亇 午 尔 布

争 勿 久

乞 名

以	似	駄	秋
by means of; datum	resemble	no good, poor quality	fall (autumn)
I	JI	DA	SHŪ
#	ni*ru*	#	aki
r 9 s 5	r 9 s 7	r 187 s 14	r 115 s 9

軌	執	就	納
track, orbit	grasp; carry out	start to	pay; obtain; store; supply
KI	SHITSU SHŪ	SHŪ JU	NŌ NA NA' NAN TO
#	to*ru*	tsu*ku*..	osa*meru*..
r 159 s 9	r 32 s 11	r 43 s 12	r 120 s 10

竹	許	称	飾
bamboo	permit	name, title	decorate
-	-	-	-
CHIKU	KYO	SHŌ	SHOKU
take	yuru*su*	#	kaza*ru*
r 118 s 6	r 149 s 11	r 115 s 10	r 184 s 13

浄	静	物	畝
pure	quiet	thing	ridge
	-		*se*
JŌ	SEI JŌ	BUTSU MOTSU	#
#	shizu shizu+	mono	une se
r 85 s 9	r 174 s 14	r 93 s 8	r 102 s 10

乾	銘		
dry	inscription		
	-		
KAN	MEI		
kawa*ku*..	#		
r 5 s 11	r 167 s 14		

丂　而　瓦

王　正

不　开

云　尸　巨

卩　巳　予　羿

丁　彐　弓　子

巧	朽	師	瓶	
skillful - KŌ taku*mi* r 48　s 5	decay - KYŪ ku*chiru* r 75　s 6	teacher; army SHI # r 50　s 10	bottle - BIN # r 98　s 11	
狂	班	征	証	
mad - KYŌ kuru*u..* r 94　s 7	squad - HAN # r 96　s 10	conquer; go to war SEI # r 60　s 8	proof, evidence SHŌ # r 149　s 12	
杯	研	併		
cup, glass HAI saka*zuki* r 75　s 8	hone, grind, polish KEN to*gu* r 112　s 9	combine, unite HEI awa*seru* r 9　s 8		
伝	転	炉	拒	距
transmit - DEN tsuta*eru..* r 9　s 6	revolve; overturn TEN koro*bu..* r 159　s 11	furnace, hearth RO # r 86　s 8	reject - KYO # r 157　s 12	distance - KYO koba*mu* r 64　s 8
卵	犯	野	解	
egg - RAN tamago r 26　s 7	crime - HAN oka*su* r 94　s 5	field; wild YA no r 166　s 11	unravel; solve KAI GE to*ku..* r 148　s 13	
幻	羽	翻	弱	好
illusion - GEN maboroshi r 52　s 4	feather, wing U ha hane r 124　s 6	flip; translate HON hiruga*eru..* r 124　s 18	weak - JAKU yowa*i..* r 57　s 10	good; fond of KŌ kono*mu* su+ r 38　s 6

■

旧	相	門	潤	欄
old, former	mutual; minister	gate, door	moisten	railing; column (in newspaper)
KYŪ	SŌ SHŌ	MON	- JUN	RAN
#	ai-	kado	uruou.. uru+	#
r 72* s 5	r 109 s 9	r 169 s 8	r 85 s 15	r 75 s 20
況	祝	損	韻	絹
conditions	celebrate	loss, harm; fail to	rhyme, tone	silk
- KYŌ	- SHUKU SHŪ	SON	IN	- KEN
#	iwau	sokonau..	#	kinu
r 85 s 8	r 113 s 7	r 64 s 13	r 180 s 19	r 120 s 13
絵	幹	蛇		
picture	trunk, main part	snake		
- E KAI	- KAN	- JA DA		
#	miki	hebi		
r 120 s 12	r 51 s 13	r 142 s 11		
託	耗	任	妊	
entrust	use up, wear out	entrust; duties	pregnant	
- TAKU	- MŌ KŌ	- NIN	- NIN	
#	#	makaseru..	#	
r 149 s 10	r 127 s 10	r 9 s 6	r 38 s 7	
訴	紙			
sue; appeal	paper			
SO	- SHI			
uttaeru	kami			
r 149 s 12	r 120 s 10			

日 目 勹

兄 員

会 全 它

壬 毛 壬

斥 氏

1	33
2	34
3	35
4	36
5	37
6	38
7	39
8	40
9	41
10	42
11	43
12	44
13	45
14	46
15	47
16	48
17	49
18	50
19	51
20	52
21	53
22	54
23	55
24	56
25	57
26	58
27	59
28	60
29	61
30	62
31	63
32	64

■ 、 ′

主	心	永	必	求	氷
master	heart	eternal	inevitable	seek, request	ice
-	-	-	-	KYŪ	HYŌ
SHU SU	SHIN	EI	HITSU	moto*meru*	kōri kō- hi
nushi omo	kokoro	naga*i*	kanara*zu*		
r 3 s 5	r 61 s 4	r 85 s 5	r 61 s 5	r 85 s 7	r 85 s 5

犬	式	弐	武	戒	我
dog	rite; style	two	military	warn; command	I, my; self; selfish
-	SHIKI	-	-	KAI	GA
KEN	#	NI	BU MU	imashi*meru*	ware wa
inu		#	#		
r 94 s 4	r 56 s 6	r 56* s 6	r 77 s 8	r 62 s 7	r 62 s 7

成	威	栽	載	裁
become; consist of	power; threat	plant	load; publish	judge; cut
SEI JŌ	I	-	SAI	SAI
na*ru*..	#	SAI	no*ru*..	saba*ku* ta+
r 62 s 6	r 38 s 9	#	r 159 s 13	r 145 s 12
		r 75 s 10		

注	泳	述	為
pour; note	swim	say	do; purpose
CHŪ	-	JUTSU	I
soso*gu*	EI	no*beru*	#
r 85 s 8	oyo*gu*	r 162 s 8	r 86* s 9
	r 85 s 8		

血	向	舟	自	白
blood	facing	boat	oneself	white
-	-	-	-	HAKU BYAKU
KETSU	KŌ	SHŪ	JI SHI	shiro*i* shiro shira-
chi	mu*kau*..	fune funa-	mizuka*ra*	
r 143 s 6	r 30 s 6	r 137 s 6	r 132 s 6	r 106 s 5

良	皇	泉	卑	鬼
good	emperor	spring; spa	lowly	demon; ghost
-	Ō KŌ	SEN	-	KI
RYŌ	#	izumi	HI	oni
yoi			iya*shii*..	
r 138 s 7	r 106 s 9	r 85 s 9	r 24 s 9	r 194 s 10

身	鳥	島	息	臭	鼻
body; self	bird	island	breath; child	stinking	nose
SHIN	-	-	child	SHŪ	BI
mi	CHŌ	TŌ	iki	kusa*i*	hana
r 158 s 7	tori	shima	r 61 s 10	r 132 s 9	r 209 s 14
	r 196 s 11	r 46 s 10			

衆	奥	楽	迫	追
the people	inmost, core	music; joy	press, urge; approach	chase; expel
-	Ō	GAKU RAKU	HAKU	TSUI
SHŪ SHU	oku	tano*shii*..	sema*ru*	ou
#	r 37 s 12	r 75 s 13	r 162 s 8	r 162 s 9
r 143 s 12				

羊	弟	兼
sheep	younger brother	combined; unable
-	TEI DAI DE	KEN
YŌ	otōto	ka*neru*
hitsuji	r 57 s 7	r 12 s 10
r 123 s 6		

半	米	券	巻
half, semi-, pen-	rice; America	ticket	roll; scroll; book
HAN	BEI MAI	-	KAN
naka*ba*.. nami	kome	KEN	maki ma+
r 24 s 5	r 119 s 6	#	r 49* s 9
		r 18 s 8	

並	益	首	前	普	慈
line up; ordinary	benefit	head, neck; chief	before	universal	compassion
HEI	-	SHU	-	-	-
nara*bu*.. nami	EKI YAKU	kubi	ZEN	FU	JI
r 1* s 8	#	r 185 s 9	mae	#	itsuku*shimu*
	r 108 s 10		r 18 s 9	r 72 s 12	r 61 s 13

羊	弟	兼
sheep	younger brother	combined; unable
-	TEI DAI DE	KEN
YŌ	otōto	ka*neru*
hitsuji	r 57 s 7	r 12 s 10
r 123 s 6		

送	逆	遂	道	遵	導
send	inverse; counter-	accomplish	way, road	comply	guide
-	GYAKU	-	DŌ TŌ	JUN	DŌ
oku*ru*	saka saka+	SUI	michi	#	michibi*ku*
r 162 s 9	r 162 s 9	to*geru*	r 162 s 12	r 162 s 15	r 41 s 15
		r 162 s 12			

羊	差	着	善
sheep	difference	arrive; wear, clothes	good
-	-	CHAKU JAKU	-
YŌ	SA	ki*ru*.. tsu+	ZEN
hitsuji	sa*su*	r 109* s 12	yo*i*
r 123 s 6	r 48 s 10		r 30 s 12

美	養	義
beauty	foster, rear	righteous; meaning; ...
-	YŌ	GI
BI	yashina*u*	#
utsuku*shii*	r 184 s 15	r 123 s 13
r 123 s 9		

八　八　人　小

八

父
father
-
FU
chichi
r 88　s 4

谷
valley
-
KOKU
tani
r 150　s 7

八

公
public;
official
KŌ
ōyake
r 12　s 4

分
portion;
minutes
BU FUN BUN
wakeru..
r 18　s 4

盆
tray
-
BON
#
r 108　s 9

貧
poverty
-
HIN BIN
mazushii
r 154　s 11

翁
old man
-
Ō
#
r 124　s 10

人

今
now
-
KIN KON
ima
r 9　s 4

合
unite;
agree; fit
GŌ GA' KA'
au..
r 30　s 6

会
meet
-
KAI E
au
r 9*　s 6

令
orders
-
REI
#
r 9　s 5

命
fate; life;
orders
MYŌ MEI
inochi
r 30　s 8

介
mediate
-
KAI
#
r 9　s 4

企
plan
-
KI
kuwadateru
r 9　s 6

全
whole
-
ZEN
mattaku
r 9*　s 6

余
remainder;
surplus
YO
amaru..
r 9　s 7

金
money; metal;
gold; Friday
KIN KON
kane kana-
r 167　s 8

舎
building,
house, hut
SHA
#
r 9*　s 8

含
include,
contain
GAN
fukumu..
r 30　s 7

念
thought;
desire
NEN
#
r 61　s 9

倉
warehouse
-
SŌ
kura
r 9　s 10

食
eat,
food
SHOKU JIKI
taberu ku+
r 184　s 9

傘
umbrella
-
SAN
kasa
r 9　s 12

途
way
-
TO
#
r 162　s 10

小

少
few
-
SHŌ
sukoshi suku+
r 42　s 4

劣
inferior
-
RETSU
otoru
r 19　s 6

省
minister; omit;
reflect upon; ...
SHŌ SEI
habuku kaeri+
r 109　s 9

単 single, simple — TAN — # — r 24* s 9

巣 nest — - — SŌ — su — r 75* s 11

挙 raise; arrest; whole; … — KYO — *ageru..* — r 64 s 10

誉 honor — - — YO — homa*re* — r 149 s 13

厳 severe — - — GEN GON — kibi*shii* ogoso+ — r 27* s 17

挙 raise; arrest; whole; … — KYO — *ageru..* — r 64 s 10

誉 honor — - — YO — homa*re* — r 149 s 13

単 single, simple — TAN — # — r 24* s 9

巣 nest — - — SŌ — su — r 75* s 11

厳 severe — - — GEN GON — kibi*shii* ogoso+ — r 27* s 17

労 labor — - — RŌ — # — r 19 s 7

栄 glory; prosper — EI — hae.. saka+ — r 75 s 9

学 study, learning — GAKU — mana*bu* — r 39 s 8

蛍 firefly — - — KEI — hotaru — r 142 s 11

営 management — - — EI — itona*mu* — r 30* s 12

覚 memorize; awake — KAKU — obo*eru* sa+ — r 147 s 12

光 light — - — KŌ — hikari hika+ — r 10 s 6

当 hit; this; applicable — TŌ — *ateru..* — r 58* s 6

肖 resemble — - — SHŌ — # — r 130 s 7

尚 respect; valued — SHŌ — # — r 42 s 8

半 half, semi-, pen- — HAN — naka*ba* — r 24 s 5

米 rice; America — BEI MAI — kome — r 119 s 6

券 ticket — - — KEN — # — r 18 s 8

巻 roll; scroll; book — KAN — maki ma+ — r 49* s 9

党 political party — TŌ — # — r 10* s 10

堂 hall; temple — DŌ — # — r 32 s 11

常 usual — - — JŌ — tsune toko- — r 50 s 11

掌 control; palm (of hand) — SHŌ — # — r 64 s 12

賞 prize — - — SHŌ — # — r 154 s 15

一

二	三	元	示	豆	言
two	three	origin	show	bean; miniature	say, speak; word
-	-	-	-	TŌ ZU	GEN GON
NI	SAN	GEN GAN	SHI JI	mame	iu koto
futa*tsu* futa	mitsu mi'+ mi	moto	shime*su*		
r 7 s 2	r 1 s 3	r 10 s 4	r 113 s 5	r 151 s 7	r 149 s 7

戸	戻	房	肩	雇	扉
door	return	room; tassel	shoulder	employ	door
-	-	BŌ	KEN	KO	HI
KO	REI	fusa	kata	yato*u*	tobira
to	modo*ru*..				
r 63 s 4	r 63 s 7	r 63 s 8	r 130 s 8	r 172 s 12	r 63 s 12

扇	遍	副	融		
fan (folding, electric)	widespread	secondary, deputy	melt, fuse; dissolve		
SEN	HEN	FUKU	YŪ		
ōgi	#	#	#		
r 63 s 10	r 162 s 12	r 18 s 11	r 142 s 16		

弐	武	頑	頭	顧	
two	military	stubborn	head; top	look back	
NI	BU MU	GAN	TŌ ZU TO	KO	
#	#	#	atama kashira	kaeri*miru*	
r 56* s 6	r 77 s 8	r 181 s 13	r 181 s 16	r 181 s 21	

丁	天	不	下		
city block; 4th; …	heaven, sky	not, un-	below, down		
CHŌ TEI	TEN	FU BU	KA GE		
#	ame ama-	#	shita moto shimo sa+ o+ kuda+		
r 1 s 2	r 37 s 4	r 1 s 4	r 1 s 3		

干	平	工	王	玉	正
dry	level; calm	industry; worker	king	jewel	correct
-	HEI BYŌ	KŌ KU	-	GYOKU	SHŌ SEI
KAN	hira tai+	#	Ō	tama	tadasu.. masa
hi*ru* ho+			#		
r 51 s 3	r 51 s 5	r 48 s 3	r 96 s 4	r 96 s 5	r 77 s 5

互	五	万	石	死	
mutual	five	ten thousand; many	stone	death	
-	-	MAN BAN	SEKI SHAKU	SHI	
GO	GO	#	ishi	shi*nu*	
taga*i*	itsu itsu+				
r 7 s 4	r 7 s 4	r 1* s 3	r 112 s 5	r 78 s 6	

夏	憂	百	面		
summer	anxiety; sorrow	hundred	face, mask		
-	YŪ	-	MEN		
KA GE	ure*eru*.. u+	HYAKU	omote omo tsura		
natsu		#			
r 34* s 10	r 61 s 15	r 106 s 6	r 176 s 9		

■▬ ー

丙	両	雨	至	否	蚕
3rd	both	rain	arrive; utmost	negate	silkworm
-	-	-	-	-	-
HEI	RYŌ	U	SHI	HI	SAN
		ame ama-	ita*ru*	ina	kaiko
#	#				
r 1 s 5	r 1* s 6	r 173 s 8	r 133 s 6	r 30 s 7	r 142 s 10

更	再	画	璽
renew; late	again; re-	picture; *kanji* stroke	imperial seal
KŌ	SAI SA	GA KAKU	JI
sara fu+	futata*bi*	#	#
r 72* s 7	r 13 s 6	r 102 s 8	r 96 s 19

雪	雲	雰	零	雷	電
snow	cloud	atmosphere	zero	thunder	electricity
-	-	-	-	-	-
SETSU	UN	FUN	REI	RAI	DEN
yuki	kumo	#	#	kaminari	#
r 173 s 11	r 173 s 12	r 173 s 12	r 173 s 13	r 173 s 13	r 173 s 13

需	霊	震	霜	露	霧
need, demand	spirit, soul	quake	frost	dew; exposed	fog
JU	REI RYŌ	SHIN	SŌ	RO RŌ	MU
#	tama	furu*eru*..	shimo	tsuyu	kiri
r 173 s 14	r 173 s 15	r 173 s 15	r 173 s 17	r 173 s 21	r 173 s 19

西	亜	耳
west	Asia; sub-	ear
-	-	-
SEI SAI	A	JI
nishi	#	mimi
r 146 s 6	r 7 s 7	r 128 s 6

要	票	覆	覇
essential	vote; chit	cover; topple	supremacy
-	-	-	-
YŌ	HYŌ	FUKU	HA
i*ru*	#	ō*u* kutsugae+	#
r 146 s 9	r 113 s 11	r 146 s 18	r 146 s 19

亜	悪	遷
Asia; sub-	bad, wicked	transition
A	AKU O	-
#	waru*i*	SEN
r 7 s 7	r 61 s 11	#
		r 162 s 15

ケ ー ヒ マ ム

ケ

| 色 color - SHIKI SHOKU iro r 139 s 6 | 免 exemption - MEN manuka*reru* r 10 s 8 | 負 defeated; bear, suffer FU ma*keru*.. o+ r 154 s 9 | 魚 fish - GYO sakana uo r 195 s 11 | 角 angle, corner KAKU kado tsuno r 148 s 7 | 争 dispute - SŌ araso*u* r 6* s 6 |
| 危 dangerous - KI abu*nai* aya+ r 26 s 6 | 象 shape; elephant SHŌ ZŌ # r 152 s 12 | 急 hurry; sudden KYŪ iso*gu* r 61 s 9 | 逸 miss, let slip; deviate; excel ITSU # r 162 s 11 | | |

一

| 冗 superfluous - JŌ # r 14 s 4 | 写 copy - SHA utsu*su*.. r 14* s 5 | 軍 army - GUN # r 159 s 9 | 冠 crown - KAN kanmuri r 14 s 9 | 欠 lack - KETSU ka*ku*.. r 76 s 4 | 運 transport; luck UN hako*bu* r 162 s 12 |

ヒ

| 気 spirit; air KI KE # r 84 s 6 | 毎 every, each MAI # r 80 s 6 | 午 noon - GO # r 24 s 4 | 年 year - NEN toshi r 51 s 6 | 缶 tin can KAN # r 121 s 6 | 矢 arrow - SHI ya r 111 s 5 |
| 無 without, -less; not be MU BU na*i* r 86 s 12 | 舞 dance - BU ma*u* mai r 136 s 15 | 欠 lack - KETSU ka*ku*.. r 76 s 4 | 行 go; do; line GYŌ KŌ AN i*ku* yu+ okona+ r 144 s 6 | | |

マ

| 予 pre-, fore-; I YO # r 6* s 4 | 矛 spear, lance MU hoko r 110 s 5 | 柔 soft - JŪ NYŪ yawa*raka*.. r 75 s 9 | 勇 courage - YŪ isa*mu* r 19 s 9 |
| 通 pass; street; commute; ... TSŪ TSU tō*ru*.. kayo+ r 162 s 10 | 了 finish; understand RYŌ # r 6 s 2 | 子 child - SHI SU ko r 39 s 3 | |

ム

| 弁 speak, debate; valve; ... BEN # r 55 s 5 | 台 pedestal; Taiwan DAI TAI # r 30* s 5 | 怠 lazy; neglect TAI okota*ru* nama+ r 61 s 9 | 参 visit; join in SAN mairu r 28 s 8 |

一 口 禾

一

千	手	毛	乏	舌	系
thousand	hand	hair, fur	scarcity; poverty	tongue	lineage; group
-	-	-	-	-	-
SEN	SHU	MŌ	BŌ	ZETSU	KEI
chi	te ta	ke	tobo*shii*	shita	#
r 24 s 3	r 64 s 4	r 82 s 4	r 4 s 4	r 135 s 6	r 120 s 7

看	番	垂	乗	重
watch over	vigil; ranking	droop	ride	heavy; layered
-	-	-	-	-
KAN	BAN	SUI	JŌ	JŪ CHŌ
#	#	ta*reru..*	no*ru..*	omo*i* kasa+ -e
r 109 s 9	r 102 s 12	r 32 s 8	r 4 s 9	r 166 s 9

口

妥	受	愛	爵
agree; calm	receive	love	peerage
-	-	-	-
DA	JU	AI	SHAKU
#	u*keru..*	#	#
r 38 s 7	r 29 s 8	r 61 s 13	r 87 s 17

禾

季	秀	委	香	番	透
season	excellent	entrust	fragrance	vigil; ranking	transparent
-	-	-	-	-	-
KI	SHŪ	I	KŌ KYŌ	BAN	TŌ
#	hii*deru*	#	ka kao+	#	su*ku..*
r 39 s 8	r 115 s 7	r 38 s 8	r 186 s 9	r 102 s 12	r 162 s 10

亠 古 古 古 白

亠

亡	立	文	交	六
deceased	stand, rise, set up	literature	intercourse	six
-	RITSU RYŪ	-	-	-
BŌ MŌ	tatsu..	BUN MON	KŌ	ROKU
nai		fumi	majiru maji+ ka+	mu mu'+ mu+ mui
r 8 s 3	r 117 s 5	r 67 s 4	r 8 s 6	r 12 s 4

方	市	衣	玄	片
direction; side; person	city; market	garment	dark; occult	part, flake; single, one-
HŌ	SHI	-	GEN	HEN
kata	ichi	l	#	kata
r 70 s 4	r 50 s 5	koromo		
		r 145 s 6	r 95 s 5	r 91 s 4

古

夜	六
night	six
-	-
YA	ROKU
yoru yo	mu mu'+ mu+ mui
r 36 s 8	r 12 s 4

古

産
give birth
-
SAN
ubu u+
r 100 s 11

古

商	高
trade	high, tall; sum
-	KŌ
SHŌ	taka taka+
akinau	r 189 s 10
r 30 s 11	

白

卒	率	畜	衰	裏	褒
graduate; soldier	ratio; leader	livestock	decline	back, rear	praise
SOTSU	SOTSU RITSU	CHIKU	SUI	RI	-
#	hikiiru	#	otoroeru	ura	HŌ
r 24 s 8	r 95 s 11	r 102 s 10	r 145 s 10	r 145 s 13	homeru
					r 145 s 15

京	哀	享	亭	豪	高
capital city	pity, grief	enjoy; receive	inn	magnificent; Australia	high, tall; sum
KYŌ KEI	AI	KYŌ	-	GŌ	KŌ
#	aware..	#	TEI	#	taka taka+
r 8 s 8	r 30 s 9	r 8 s 8	#	r 152 s 14	r 189 s 10
			r 8 s 9		

言
say, speak; word
GEN GON
iu koto
r 149 s 7

■ 宮亠兯峦 音

宮	京	哀	享	亭	豪	高
	capital city	pity, grief	enjoy; receive	inn	magnificent; Australia	high, tall; sum
	KYŌ KEI	AI	KYŌ	TEI	GŌ	KŌ
	#	aware..	#	#	#	taka taka+
	r 8 s 8	r 30 s 9	r 8 s 8	r 8 s 9	r 152 s 14	r 189 s 10

亠	忘	妄	盲
	forget	reckless	blind
	-	-	-
	BŌ	MŌ BŌ	MŌ
	wasureru	#	#
	r 61 s 7	r 38 s 6	r 109 s 8

兯	充	育	棄
	allot; fill	bring up (child)	abandon
	JŪ	IKU	KI
	ateru	sodateru..	#
	r 10 s 6	r 130 s 8	r 75 s 13

峦	斉	斎
	equal	purify; abstain from
	-	
	SEI	SAI
	#	#
	r 67* s 8	r 67* s 11

峦	変	恋	蛮
	alter; odd	romantic love	barbarian
	HEN	REN	-
	kawaru..	koi ko+ koi+	BAN
	r 34* s 9	r 61 s 10	#
			r 142 s 12

音	辛	音	章	意	竜	童
	spicy; hardship	sound	chapter; badge	intent; mind	dragon	child
	SHIN	ON IN	SHŌ	I	RYŪ	DŌ
	karai	oto ne	#	#	tatsu	warabe
	r 160 s 7	r 180 s 9	r 117 s 11	r 61 s 13	r 117* s 10	r 117 s 12

帝	産	商	適
emperor	give birth	trade	suitable
-		-	-
TEI	SAN	SHŌ	TEKI
#	ubu u+	akinau	#
r 50 s 9	r 100 s 11	r 30 s 11	r 162 s 14

穴	守	安	宅	宇	字
hole	protect	calm; cheap	home	cosmos	character, *kanji*, word
-	-	AN	-	U	JI
KETSU	SHU SU	yasu*i*	TAKU	#	aza
ana	mori mamo+		#	#	r 39 s 6
r 116 s 5	r 40 s 6	r 40 s 6	r 40 s 6	r 40 s 6	

家	実	宝	定
house; family	real, true; bear fruit	treasure	fix, decide
KA KE	JITSU	-	TEI JŌ
ie ya	mi mino+	HŌ	sada*meru..*
r 40 s 10	r 40 s 8	takara	r 40 s 8
		r 40 s 8	

宙	宜	官
sky, (outer) space	suitable; best wishes	official; government
CHŪ	GI	KAN
#	#	#
r 40 s 8	r 40 s 8	r 40 s 8

穴	宿	寝	寂	窃	窮
hole	inn, lodge	sleep	lonely	steal	extreme
-	SHUKU	-	JAKU SEKI	-	-
KETSU	yado yado+	SHIN	sabi sabi+	SETSU	KYŪ
ana	r 40 s 11	ne*ru..*	r 40 s 11	#	kiwa*maru..*
r 116 s 5		r 40 s 13		r 116 s 9	r 116 s 15

守
protect
-
SHU SU
mori mamo+
r 40 s 6

宀

宰	害	憲	案	寄	宵
supervise, manage	harm	the law, constitution	plan	approach; give	dusk
SAI	- GAI	- KEN	- AN	KI	- SHŌ
#	#	#	#	yo*ru*..	yoi
r 40 s 10	r 40 s 10	r 61 s 16	r 75 s 10	r 40 s 11	r 40 s 10

寒	寛	容	寧	密
cold	tolerant	looks; contain	calm	secret; dense; delicate
- KAN	- KAN	- YŌ	- NEI	MITSU
samu*i*	#	#	#	#
r 40 s 12	r 40 s 13	r 40 s 10	r 40 s 14	r 40 s 11

審	客	察	寮
trial	guest, customer	inspect; guess	hostel, dormitory
- SHIN	KYAKU KAKU	- SATSU	RYŌ
#	#	#	-
r 40 s 15	r 40 s 9	r 40 s 14	r 40 s 15

官	宮	室	宴	賓	寡
official; government	shrine, palace	room	banquet	guest	few; widow
KAN	KYŪ GŪ KU	- SHITSU	- EN	- HIN	- KA
#	miya	muro	#	#	#
r 40 s 8	r 40 s 10	r 40 s 9	r 40 s 10	r 154 s 15	r 40 s 14

宮

完	宗	宣	富
complete; perfect	religion	announce	wealth
KAN	- SHŪ SŌ	- SEN	- FU FŪ
#	#	#	tomi to+
r 40 s 7	r 40 s 8	r 40 s 9	r 40 s 12

室	賓	寡
room	guest	few; widow
- SHITSU	- HIN	KA
muro	#	#
r 40 s 9	r 154 s 15	r 40 s 14

穴

空	究	突	容
air, sky; empty	research, investigate	thrust	looks; contain
KŪ	KYŪ	- TOTSU	YŌ
sora a+ kara	kiwa*meru*	tsu*ku*	#
r 116 s 8	r 116 s 7	r 116 s 8	r 40 s 10

窓	窒	窯	窃	窮
window	suffocate; plug	kiln	steal	extreme
- SŌ	- CHITSU	- YŌ	- SETSU	- KYŪ
mado	#	kama	#	kiwa*maru*..
r 116 s 11	r 116 s 11	r 116 s 15	r 116 s 9	r 116 s 15

芝 turf - # shiba r 140 s 6	**芋** potato - # imo r 140 s 6	**英** talented; English EI # r 140 s 8	**苗** seedling - BYŌ nae nawa r 140 s 8	**茂** luxuriant, overgrown MO shige*ru* r 140 s 8	**芽** bud - GA me r 140 s 8
芳 fragrant; (honorific) your HŌ kanba*shii* r 140 s 7	**荒** wild - KŌ ara*i* a+ r 140 s 9	**苦** pain; bitter KU kuru*shii*.. niga+ r 140 s 8	**若** young - JAKU NYAKU waka*i* mo+ r 140 s 8	**華** gorgeous; flowery; China KA KE hana r 140 s 10	

花 flower - KA hana r 140 s 7	**荘** villa; sublime SŌ # r 140 s 9	**荷** load, cargo KA ni r 140 s 10			
落 fall, drop RAKU o*tosu*.. r 140 s 12	**藩** clan - HAN # r 140 s 18	**藻** seaweed - SŌ mo r 140 s 19	**薄** dilute, thin HAKU usu*i*.. r 140 s 16	**薪** firewood - SHIN takigi r 140 s 16	

若 young - JAKU NYAKU waka*i* mo+ r 140 s 8	**薦** recommend - SEN susu*meru* r 140 s 16	**著** author; notable CHO arawa*su* ichijiru+ r 140 s 11

菊 chrysan- themum KIKU # r 140 s 11	**茂** luxuriant, overgrown MO shige*ru* r 140 s 8

蔵 store, keep ZŌ kura r 140 s 15	**繭** cocoon - KEN mayu r 120 s 18

菌 germ; fungi KIN # r 140 s 11

苩

苦 pain; bitter / KU / kurushii.. niga+ / r 140 s 8	芳 fragrant; (honorific) your / - / HŌ / kanbashii / r 140 s 7	荒 wild / - / KŌ / arai a+ / r 140 s 9	蓄 amass / - / CHIKU / takuwaeru / r 140 s 13	著 author; notable / CHO / arawasu ichijiru+ / r 140 s 11	
茶 tea / - / CHA SA / # / r 140 s 9	菜 vegetable / - / SAI / na / r 140 s 11	葉 leaf / - / YŌ / ha / r 140 s 12	薬 medicine, drug / YAKU / kusuri / r 140 s 16	薫 fragrant / - / KUN / kaoru / r 140 s 16	
芸 art, skill / GEI / # / r 140 s 7	芽 bud / - / GA / me / r 140 s 8	茎 stalk, stem / KEI / kuki / r 140 s 8	葬 bury; funeral / SŌ / hōmuru / r 140 s 12	蒸 steam; sultry / JŌ / musu.. / r 140 s 13	華 gorgeous; flowery; China / KA KE / hana / r 140 s 10
草 grass, plants / SŌ / kusa / r 140 s 9	墓 grave, tomb / BO / haka / r 32 s 13	幕 curtain; act (of play) / MAKU BAKU / # / r 50 s 13	慕 adore; yearn / BO / shitau / r 61 s 14	募 raise funds, recruit / BO / tsunoru / r 19 s 12	暮 live; end; dusk / BO / kureru.. / r 72 s 14
菓 candy, cake / KA / # / r 140 s 11	夢 dream / - / MU / yume / r 36 s 13				
共 together; co- / KYŌ / tomo / r 12 s 6	昔 ancient / - / SEKI SHAKU / mukashi / r 72 s 8	恭 respect / - / KYŌ / uyauyashii / r 61 s 10	黄 yellow / - / KŌ Ō / ki ko- / r 201 s 11	曹 lawyer; companion / SŌ / # / r 72* s 11	遭 encounter / - / SŌ / au / r 162 s 14
井 well (for water) / SEI SHŌ / i / r 7 s 4	甘 sweet / - / KAN / amai.. / r 99 s 5	某 a certain (eg person) / BŌ / # / r 75 s 9	革 leather; reform / KAKU / kawa / r 177 s 9	鼓 drum / - / KO / tsuzumi / r 207 s 13	賛 praise, approve / SAN / # / r 154 s 15

十　土　士

土
soil, land;
Saturday
DO TO
tsuchi
r 32　s 3

士
warrior;
man
SHI
#
r 33　s 3

古
old,
antiquated
KO
furu*i..*
r 30　s 5

克
overcome
-
KOKU
#
r 10　s 7

支
branch;
support
SHI
sasa*eru*
r 65　s 4

市
city;
market
SHI
ichi
r 50　s 5

直
directly;
fix
CHOKU JIKI
nao*su..* tada+
r 109　s 8

真
true
-
SHIN
ma
r 109　s 10

索
cord;
seek
SAKU
#
r 120　s 10

南
south
-
NAN NA
minami
r 24　s 9

喪
mourning
-
SŌ
mo
r 30　s 12

衷
inmost
-
CHŪ
#
r 2*　s 9

束
bundle
-
SOKU
taba
r 75　s 7

東
east
-
TŌ
higashi
r 75　s 8

車
vehicle
-
SHA
kuruma
r 159　s 7

恵
favor,
kindness
KEI E
megu*mu*
r 61　s 10

専
exclusive
-
SEN
moppa*ra*
r 41　s 9

事
thing,
matter
JI ZU
koto
r 6　s 8

妻
wife
-
SAI
tsuma
r 38　s 8

土

去
depart;
past, gone
KYO KO
sa*ru*
r 28　s 5

寺
temple
-
JI
tera
r 41　s 6

走
run
-
SŌ
hashi*ru*
r 156　s 7

赤
red
-
SEKI SHAKU
aka aka+
r 155　s 7

幸
happiness,
good fortune
KŌ
saiwa*i* shiawa+ sachi
r 51　s 8

遠
distant
-
EN ON
tō*i*
r 162　s 13

達
achieve
-
TATSU
#
r 162　s 12

士

吉
lucky
-
KICHI KITSU
#
r 30　s 6

壱
one
-
ICHI
#
r 32*　s 7

売
sell
-
BAI
u*ru..*
r 32*　s 7

声
voice
-
SEI SHŌ
koe kowa-
r 32*　s 7

志
aspire,
intend
SHI
kokorozashi kokoroza+
r 61　s 7

喜
rejoice
-
KI
yoroko*bu*
r 30　s 12

古
old
-
KO
furu*i..*
r 30　s 5

克
overcome
-
KOKU
#
r 10　s 7

支
branch;
support
SHI
sasa*eru*
r 65　s 4

■□ 書 考 ├ 止 共 山

毒	青	責	素	表	麦
poison	blue, green; young	blame; duty	basic, bare	surface; chart; display	cereal
-	SEI SHŌ	SEKI	SO SU	HYŌ	BAKU
DOKU	ao ao+	se*meru*	-	omote arawa+	mugi
#			#		
r 80 s 8	r 174 s 8	r 154 s 11	r 120 s 10	r 145 s 8	r 199 s 7

老	考	孝	者	煮	
old age	consider	filial piety	person	boil, cook	
-	-	-	-	-	
RŌ	KŌ	KŌ	SHA	SHA	
oi*ru* fu+	kanga*eru*	#	mono	nie*ru*..	
r 125 s 6	r 125 s 6	r 39 s 7	r 125 s 8	r 86 s 12	

占	点	卓	貞
divination; occupy	point, dot	eminent; desk	chastity
SEN	TEN	TAKU	TEI
urana*u* shi+	#	#	#
r 25 s 5	r 86* s 9	r 24 s 8	r 154 s 9

与	上
give	above, up
-	-
YO	JŌ SHŌ
ata*eru*	ue kami uwa- a+ nobo+
r 1* s 3	r 1 s 3

虐	虚	虞	虜	慮	膚
cruel	void	anxiety	captive	consider; concern for	skin
-	KYO KO	-	RYO	RYO	FU
GYAKU	#	#	#	#	#
shiita*geru*		osore			
r 141 s 9	r 141 s 11	r 141 s 13	r 141 s 13	r 61 s 15	r 130 s 15

歩	肯	歯	歳
walk	agreement	tooth	year, years old
-	KŌ	-	SAI SEI
HO BU FU	#	SHI	#
aru*ku* ayu+		ha	
r 77 s 8	r 130 s 8	r 77* s 12	r 77 s 13

共	昔	恭	黄
together; co-	ancient	respect	yellow
KYŌ	SEKI SHAKU	KYŌ	KŌ Ō
tomo	mukashi	uyauya*shii*	ki ko-
r 12 s 6	r 72 s 8	r 61 s 10	r 201 s 11

岩	炭	岸	崇	崩	出
rock, boulder	charcoal	shore	venerate	crumble	go out, exit; put out
GAN	-	GAN	-	-	SHUTSU SUI
iwa	TAN	kishi	SŪ	HŌ	de*ru* da+
	sumi		#	kuzu*reru*..	
r 46 s 8	r 86 s 9	r 46 s 8	r 46 s 11	r 46 s 11	r 17 s 5

1	33
2	34
3	35
4	36
5	37
6	38
7	39
8	**40**
9	41
10	42
11	43
12	44
13	45
14	46
15	47
16	48
17	49
18	50
19	51
20	52
21	53
22	54
23	55
24	56
25	57
26	58
27	59
28	60
29	61
30	62
31	63
32	64

夂 大 夫 关 木

夂

各	冬	条	多	名
each	winter	clause	many	name; fame
-	-	-	-	MEI MYŌ
KAKU	TŌ	JŌ	TA	na
onoono	fuyu	#	ōi	
r 30　s 6	r 15　s 5	r 75　s 7	r 36　s 6	r 30　s 6

大

奇	奔	奪	奮	太
strange	hurry	snatch, rob	inspired, excited	thick; great
-	-	DATSU	FUN	TA TAI
KI	HON	ubau	furuu	futoi..
#	#			
r 37　s 8	r 37　s 8	r 37　s 14	r 37　s 16	r 37　s 4

夫

奉	奏	泰	春	寿
offering; respectful	play music	tranquil	springtime	longevity
HŌ BU	-	-	-	-
tatematsuru	SŌ	TAI	SHUN	JU
	kanaderu	#	haru	kotobuki
r 37　s 8	r 37　s 9	r 85　s 10	r 72　s 9	r 41*　s 7

关

巻	券
roll; scroll; book	ticket
KAN	-
maki ma+	KEN
	#
r 49*　s 9	r 18　s 8

木

査	森
investigate	forest
-	-
SA	SHIN
#	mori
r 75　s 9	r 75　s 12

習	翌	翼
learn	next	wing
-	-	-
SHŪ	YOKU	YOKU
nara*u*	#	tsubasa
r 124　s 11	r 124　s 11	r 124　s 17

笛	笑	策	筆	第	篤
flute	laugh	plan, policy	writing brush	Number (as in 'Number 3')	good; seriously
-	-	SAKU	HITSU	DAI	TOKU
TEKI	SHŌ	#	fude	#	#
fue	wara*u* e+				
r 118　s 11	r 118　s 10	r 118　s 12	r 118　s 12	r 118　s 11	r 118　s 16

答	管	等	算	築	符
answer	pipe; control	etc; equal; grade	calculate	construct, build	symbol; tag
-	KAN	TŌ	SAN	CHIKU	FU
TŌ	kuda	hito*shii*	#	kizu*ku*	#
kota*e*..					
r 118　s 12	r 118　s 14	r 118　s 12	r 118　s 14	r 118　s 16	r 118　s 11

箱	節	範	筋	籍	簿
box	node, joint; season; …	model; norm; range	muscle, sinew	registration	record book
#	SETSU SECHI	HAN	KIN	SEKI	BO
hako	fushi	#	suji	#	#
r 118　s 15	r 118　s 13	r 118　s 15	r 118　s 12	r 118　s 20	r 118　s 19

簡	筒	箇	解	質	
simple, brief	tube	item	unravel; solve	quality; hostage	
KAN	-	-	KAI GE	SHITSU SHICHI CHI	
#	TŌ	KA	to*ku*..	#	
	tsutsu	#			
r 118　s 18	r 118　s 12	r 118　s 14	r 148　s 13	r 154　s 15	

焦	集	隻	進
scorch; hasty	gather	one (of a pair)	advance
SHŌ	SHŪ	SEKI	-
ko*gasu*.. ase+	tsudo*u* atsu+	#	SHIN
r 86　s 12	r 172　s 12	r 172　s 10	susu*mu*..
			r 162　s 11

雪	雲	霧	零	雷	電
snow	cloud	atmosphere	zero	thunder	electricity
-	-	-	-	-	-
SETSU	UN	FUN	REI	RAI	DEN
yuki	kumo	#	#	kaminari	#
r 173　s 11	r 173　s 12	r 173　s 12	r 173　s 13	r 173　s 13	r 173　s 13

需	霊	震	霜	露	霧
need, demand	spirit, soul	quake	frost	dew; exposed	fog
JU	REI RYŌ	SHIN	-	RO RŌ	MU
#	tama	furu*eru*..	SŌ	tsuyu	kiri
			shimo		
r 173　s 14	r 173　s 15	r 173　s 17	r 173　s 17	r 173　s 21	r 173　s 19

1	33
2	34
3	35
4	36
5	37
6	38
7	39
8	40
9	**41**
10	42
11	43
12	44
13	45
14	46
15	47
16	48
17	49
18	50
19	51
20	52
21	53
22	54
23	55
24	56
25	57
26	58
27	59
28	60
29	61
30	62
31	63
32	64

口

兄	号	呈	足
elder brother	number, designation	presentation	foot, leg; suffice
KEI KYŌ	GŌ	-	SOKU
ani	#	TEI	ashi ta+
r 10 s 5	r 30* s 5	#	r 157 s 7
		r 30 s 8	

品	呉	員
goods; grace	give; *Wu*	member
HIN	GO	-
shina	#	!N
r 30 s 9	r 30 s 7	#
		r 30 s 10

日

早	昇	星	是	易	冒
early, swift	rise	star	right, just; this	easy; trade; divination	risk; defy
SŌ SA'	SHŌ	SEI SHŌ	ZE	EKI I	BŌ
hayai..	noboru	hoshi	#	yasashii	okasu
r 72 s 6	r 72 s 8	r 72 s 9	r 72 s 9	r 72 s 8	r 109* s 9

昆	晶	最	暑	景	暴
insect	crystal	utmost	hot weather, summer	scenery	violent
-	-	-	SHO	KEI	-
KON	SHŌ	SAI	atsui	#	BŌ BAKU
#	#	mottomo			abareru..
r 72 s 8	r 72 s 12	r 72* s 12	r 72 s 12	r 72 s 12	r 72 s 15

量	曇	皇	泉
quantity	cloudy	emperor	spring; spa
-	DON	Ō KŌ	SEN
RYŌ	kumoru	#	izumi
hakaru	r 72 s 16	r 106 s 9	r 85 s 9
r 166 s 12			

目

貝	具	見	県	且
shell; money	tool	see	prefecture	moreover, besides
#	-	-	-	#
kai	GU	KEN	KEN	katsu
r 154 s 7	#	miru..	#	r 1 s 5
	r 12 s 8	r 147 s 7	r 109* s 9	

身	臭	鼻
body; self	stinking	nose
SHIN	-	-
mi	SHŪ	BI
r 158 s 7	kusai	hana
	r 132 s 9	r 209 s 14

中

忠	患	貴	遺	遣
loyalty	ill	noble, valued	bequeath	send; spend; use
-	-	KI	-	KEN
CHŪ	KAN	tattoi.. tōto+	I YUI	tsukau..
#	wazurau	r 154 s 12	#	r 162 s 13
r 61 s 8	r 61 s 11		r 162 s 15	

田

果	男	思	累	界	胃
fruit, result	male	think	accumulate	world; scope	stomach
KA	- DAN NAN	- SHI	- RUI	KAI	- I
ha*tasu*..	otoko	omo*u*	#	#	#
r 75 s 8	r 102 s 7	r 61 s 9	r 120 s 11	r 102 s 9	r 130 s 9

甲	里	畳	異	黒	愚
1st; shell	village; *ri*	fold up; *tatami* mat	different	black	foolish
KŌ KAN	RI	JŌ	I	KOKU	GU
#	sato	tatami tata+	koto koto+	kuro kuro+	oro*ka*
r 102 s 5	r 166 s 7	r 102 s 12	r 102 s 11	r 203 s 11	r 61 s 13

塁	墨	遇	卑	鬼	貫
fort; base (baseball)	India ink	meet; deal with	lowly	demon; ghost	pierce; carry through
RUI	BOKU	GŪ	- HI	KI	KAN
#	sumi	#	iya*shii*..	oni	tsuran*uku*
r 32 s 12	r 32 s 14	r 162 s 12	r 24 s 9	r 194 s 10	r 154 s 11

四

罪	買	置	署
crime	buy	put, place	signature; (police) station
- ZAI	- BAI	- CHI	SHO
tsumi	ka*u*	o*ku*	#
r 122 s 13	r 154 s 12	r 122 s 13	r 122 s 13

罰	羅	罷	還	衆	皿
punishment	net, gauze	stop work	return	the people	dish
- BATSU BACHI	RA	- HI	- KAN	SHŪ SHU	-
#	#	#	#	#	sara
r 122 s 14	r 122 s 19	r 122 s 15	r 162 s 16	r 143 s 12	r 108 s 5

西

要	票	覆	覇
essential	vote; chit	cover; topple	supremacy
- YŌ	HYŌ	FUKU	HA
i*ru*	#	ō*u* kutsugae+	#
r 146 s 9	r 113 s 11	r 146 s 18	r 146 s 19

亜	悪	遷
Asia; sub-	bad, wicked	transition
A	AKU O	- SEN
#	waru*i*	#
r 7 s 7	r 61 s 11	r 162 s 15

旨	帯	貴	遺	遣
gist	belt, sash; wear; zone	noble, valued	bequeath	send; spend; use
-			-	
SHI	TAI	KI	I YUI	KEN
mune	obi o+	tatto*i*.. tōto+	#	tsuka*u*..
r 72 s 6	r 50 s 10	r 154 s 12	r 162 s 15	r 162 s 13

粛	告	先	脅	炎
solemn; purge	notify, announce	ahead; previous	threaten	inflame
SHUKU	KOKU	SEN	KYŌ	EN
#	tsu*geru*	saki	obiya*kasu* odo+	honō
r 129 s 11	r 30 s 7	r 10 s 6	r 130 s 10	r 86 s 8

皇	泉	息	臭	鼻
emperor	spring; spa	breath; child	stinking	nose
-			-	-
ŌKŌ	SEN	SOKU	SHŪ	BI
#	izumi	iki	kusa*i*	hana
r 106 s 9	r 85 s 9	r 61 s 10	r 132 s 9	r 209 s 14

卑	鬼	衆
lowly	demon; ghost	the people
-		
HI	KI	SHŪ SHU
iya*shii*..	oni	#
r 24 s 9	r 194 s 10	r 143 s 12

革	某	基	碁	甚
leather; reform	a certain (eg person)	foundations	*go* (the board game)	extremely
KAKU	BŌ	KI	GO	-
kawa	#	moto motoi	#	JIN
r 177 s 9	r 75 s 9	r 32 s 11	r 112 s 13	hanaha*da*..
				r 99 s 9

業	典	豊	農	曹
business; deed, act	reference book	abundant	farming	lawyer; companion
GYŌ GŌ	TEN	-	-	SŌ
waza	#	HŌ	NŌ	#
r 75 s 13	r 12 s 8	yuta*ka*	#	r 72* s 11
		r 151 s 13	r 161 s 13	

多	名	無	舞
many	name; fame	without, -less; not be	dance
-			-
TA	MEI MYŌ	MU BU	BU
ō*i*	na	na*i*	ma*u* mai
r 36 s 6	r 30 s 6	r 86 s 12	r 136 s 15

災	希	凶
disaster	rare; wish	misfortune; evil
-		
SAI	KI	KYŌ
wazawa*i*	#	#
r 86 s 7	r 50 s 7	r 17 s 4

⼯不天云

貢	否	蚕	至
tribute	negate	silkworm	arrive; utmost
-	-	-	-
KŌ KU	HI	SAN	SHI
mitsu*gu*	ina	kaiko	ita*ru*
r 154 s 10	r 30 s 7	r 142 s 10	r 133 s 6

亜百凸毌

悪	夏	憂	骨	貫
bad, wicked	summer	anxiety; sorrow	bone	pierce; carry through
AKU O	KA GE	YŪ	- KOTSU	KAN
waru*i*	natsu	ure*eru*.. u+	hone	tsuranu*ku*
r 61 s 11	r 34* s 10	r 61 s 15	r 188 s 10	r 154 s 11

又己刀刃

桑	忌	召	忍
mulberry	mourn; abhor	summon	endure; conceal
SŌ	KI	SHŌ	NIN
kuwa	*imu*..	me*su*	shinobu..
r 75 s 10	r 61 s 7	r 30 s 5	r 61 s 7

彐聿尹巨

尋	粛	君	長
inquire; normal	solemn; purge	lord; you	long; chief
JIN	SHUKU	KUN	CHŌ
tazu*neru*	#	kimi	naga*i*
r 41 s 12	r 129 s 11	r 30 s 7	r 168 s 8

王幺非

兵	岳	糸	輩	悲
soldier	mountain peak	thread	fellow, companion	sad
HEI HYŌ	GAKU	- SHI	HAI	- HI
#	take	ito	#	kana*shii*..
r 12 s 7	r 46 s 8	r 120 s 6	r 159 s 15	r 61 s 12

臼匕マ乂几

児	疑	殺
child	doubt	kill
- JI NI	- GI	- SATSU SETSU SAI
#	utaga*u*	koro*su*
r 10 s 7	r 103 s 14	r 79 s 10

癶癶所

祭	登	発	質
festival	climb	emit; start	quality; hostage
- SAI	- TŌ TO	HATSU HOTSU	SHITSU SHICHI CHI
matsu*ru*..	nobo*ru*	#	#
r 113 s 11	r 105 s 12	r 105 s 9	r 154 s 15

立丽日日己

競	麗	器	選
compete	beautiful	container; utensil; skill	select
KYŌ KEI	- REI	KI	SEN
kiso*u* se+	uruwa*shii*	utsuwa	era*bu*
r 117 s 20	r 198 s 19	r 30 s 15	r 162 s 15

1	33
2	34
3	35
4	36
5	37
6	38
7	39
8	40
9	41
10	42
11	**43**
12	44
13	45
14	46
15	47
16	48
17	49
18	50
19	51
20	52
21	53
22	54
23	55
24	56
25	57
26	58
27	59
28	60
29	61
30	62
31	63
32	64

少	歩	抄	秒	妙	砂
few	walk	excerpt	second (unit of time)	miraculous; odd	sand
-	-	-	-	-	-
SHŌ	HO BU FU	SHŌ	BYŌ	MYŌ	SA SHA
suko*shi* suku+	aru*ku* ayu+	#	#	#	suna
r 42 s 4	r 77 s 8	r 64 s 7	r 115 s 9	r 38 s 7	r 112 s 9

参
visit; join in
SAN
mai*ru*
r 28 s 8

太	勺	寸	冬	尽	寒
thick; great	*shaku*	tiny	winter	exhaust	cold
TA TAI	SHAKU	SUN	TŌ	JIN	KAN
futo*i*..	#	#	fuyu	tsu*kusu*..	samu*i*
r 37 s 4	r 20 s 3	r 41 s 3	r 15 s 5	r 44* s 6	r 40 s 12

守	寿	等	寺	専	尊
protect	longevity	etc; equal; grade	temple	exclusive	esteem; your
-	-	-	-	-	-
SHU SU	JU	TŌ	JI	SEN	SON
mori mamo+	kotobuki	hito*shii*	tera	mopp*ara*	tatto*i*.. tōto+
r 40 s 6	r 41* s 7	r 118 s 12	r 41 s 6	r 41 s 9	r 41 s 12

奪	尋	導	辱
snatch, rob	inquire; normal	guide	disgrace, insult
DATSU	JIN	-	JOKU
uba*u*	tazu*neru*	DŌ	hazukashi*meru*
r 37 s 14	r 41 s 12	michibi*ku*	r 161 s 10
		r 41 s 15	

冬	尽	寒
winter	exhaust	cold
-	-	-
TŌ	JIN	KAN
fuyu	tsu*kusu*..	samu*i*
r 15 s 5	r 44* s 6	r 40 s 12

共 together; co- KYŌ tomo r 12 s 6	兵 soldier - HEI HYŌ # r 12 s 7	呉 give; *Wu* GO # r 30 s 7	穴 hole - KETSU ana r 116 s 5	六 six - ROKU mu mu'+ mu+ mui r 12 s 4	
貝 shell; money # kai r 154 s 7	具 tool - GU # r 12 s 8	典 reference book TEN # r 12 s 8			
真 true - SHIN ma r 109 s 10	黄 yellow - KŌ Ō ki ko- r 201 s 11	異 different - I koto koto+ r 102 s 11	翼 wing - YOKU tsubasa r 124 s 17	興 prosper; fun KYŌ KŌ okoru.. r 134 s 16	
貞 chastity - TEI # r 154 s 9	負 defeated; bear, suffer FU makeru.. o+ r 154 s 9	貢 tribute - KŌ KU mitsugu r 154 s 10	員 member - IN # r 30 s 10	買 buy - BAI kau r 154 s 12	
貴 noble, valued KI tattoi.. tōto+ r 154 s 12	貫 pierce; carry through KAN tsuranuku r 154 s 11	責 blame; duty SEKI semeru r 154 s 11	費 cost - HI tsuiyasu.. r 154 s 12	賞 prize - SHŌ # r 154 s 15	賓 guest - HIN # r 154 s 15
貧 poverty - HIN BIN mazushii r 154 s 11	貨 goods; coin, money KA # r 154 s 11	貸 lend, rent out TAI kasu r 154 s 12	賃 fee, wages CHIN # r 154 s 13	資 assets - SHI # r 154 s 13	
賛 praise, approve SAN # r 154 s 15	賀 good wishes - GA # r 154 s 12	貿 trade - BŌ # r 154 s 12	賢 wise - KEN kashikoi r 154 s 16	質 quality; hostage SHITSU SHICHI CHI # r 154 s 15	
欠 lack - KETSU kaku.. r 76 s 4	久 long time - KYŪ KU hisashii r 4 s 3	英 talented; English EI # r 140 s 8	肉 meat, flesh NIKU # r 130 s 6	腐 rot - FU kusaru.. r 130 s 14	虞 anxiety - # osore r 141 s 13

1	33
2	34
3	35
4	36
5	37
6	38
7	39
8	40
9	41
10	42
11	43
12	**44**
13	45
14	46
15	47
16	48
17	49
18	50
19	51
20	52
21	53
22	54
23	55
24	56
25	57
26	58
27	59
28	60
29	61
30	62
31	63
32	64

■ 儿 几 廾 匕

儿	元 origin - GEN GAN moto r 10 s 4	光 light - KŌ hikari hika+ r 10 s 6	先 ahead; previous SEN saki r 10 s 6	児 child - JI NI # r 10 s 7	兄 elder brother KEI KYŌ ani r 10 s 5	見 see - KEN miru.. r 147 s 7
	克 overcome - KOKU # r 10 s 7	充 allot; fill JŪ ateru r 10 s 6	完 complete; perfect KAN # r 40 s 7	売 sell - BAI uru.. r 32* s 7	党 political party TŌ # r 10* s 10	免 exemption - MEN manukareru r 10 s 8
	覚 memorize; awake KAKU oboeru sa+ r 147 s 12	寛 tolerant - KAN # r 40 s 13	覧 look at - RAN # r 147 s 17	穴 hole - KETSU ana r 116 s 5	冗 superfluous - JŌ # r 14 s 4	英 talented; English EI # r 140 s 8
	冠 crown - KAN kanmuri r 14 s 9	鬼 demon; ghost KI oni r 194 s 10	荒 wild - KŌ arai a+ r 140 s 9	発 emit; start HATSU HOTSU # r 105 s 9	廃 obsolete, waste, scrap HAI sutareru.. r 53 s 12	魔 demon, devil MA # r 194 s 21
几	介 mediate - KAI # r 9 s 4	界 world; scope KAI # r 102 s 9	斉 equal - SEI # r 67* s 8	斎 purify; abstain from SAI # r 67* s 11	粛 solemn; purge SHUKU # r 129 s 11	
廾	弁 speak, debate; valve; ... BEN # r 55 s 5	升 sho; measure SHŌ masu r 24 s 4	昇 rise - SHŌ noboru r 72 s 8	奔 hurry - HON # r 37 s 8	算 calculate - SAN # r 118 s 14	鼻 nose - BI hana r 209 s 14
	葬 bury; funeral SŌ hōmuru r 140 s 12	弊 evil; our/my humble HEI # r 55 s 15	戒 warn; command KAI imashimeru r 62 s 7	開 open - KAI akeru.. hira+ r 169 s 12	発 emit; start HATSU HOTSU # r 105 s 9	廃 obsolete, waste, scrap HAI sutareru.. r 53 s 12
匕	壱 one - ICHI # r 32* s 7	老 old age - RŌ oiru fu+ r 125 s 6	尼 nun - NI ama r 44 s 5			

寸

守	寿	等	寺	専	尊
protect - SHU SU mori mamo+ r 40 s 6	longevity - JU kotobuki r 41* s 7	etc; equal; grade TŌ hitoshii r 118 s 12	temple - JI tera r 41 s 6	exclusive - SEN moppara r 41 s 9	esteem; your SON tattoi.. tōto+ r 41 s 12

奪	尋	導	辱
snatch, rob DATSU ubau r 37 s 14	inquire; normal JIN tazuneru r 41 s 12	guide - DŌ michibiku r 41 s 15	disgrace, insult JOKU hazukashimeru r 161 s 10

十

千	午	干	革	卑
thousand - SEN chi r 24 s 3	noon - GO # r 24 s 4	dry - KAN hiru ho+ r 51 s 3	leather; reform KAKU kawa r 177 s 9	lowly - HI iyashii.. r 24 s 9

卒	率	辛	宰	幸
graduate; soldier SOTSU # r 24 s 8	ratio; leader SOTSU RITSU hikiiru r 95 s 11	spicy; hardship SHIN karai r 160 s 7	supervise, manage SAI # r 40 s 10	happiness, good fortune KŌ saiwai shiawa+ sachi r 51 s 8

早	卓	草	単	章
early, swift SŌ SA' hayai.. r 72 s 6	eminent; desk TAKU # r 24 s 8	grass, plants SŌ kusa r 140 s 9	single, simple TAN # r 24* s 9	chapter; badge SHŌ # r 117 s 11

傘	華	準	軍	輩
umbrella - SAN kasa r 9 s 12	gorgeous; flowery; China KA KE hana r 140 s 10	norm; quasi- JUN # r 85 s 13	army - GUN # r 159 s 9	fellow, companion HAI # r 159 s 15

巾

市	帝	帯	常	幕	幣
city; market SHI ichi r 50 s 5	emperor - TEI # r 50 s 9	belt, sash; wear; zone TAI obi o+ r 50 s 10	usual - JŌ tsune toko- r 50 s 11	curtain; act (of play) MAKU BAKU # r 50 s 13	money - HEI # r 50 s 15

布	希	席
cloth; spread FU nuno r 50 s 5	rare; wish KI # r 50 s 7	seat, place SEKI # r 50 s 10

1	33
2	34
3	35
4	36
5	37
6	38
7	39
8	40
9	41
10	42
11	43
12	44
13	**45**
14	46
15	47
16	48
17	49
18	50
19	51
20	52
21	53
22	54
23	55
24	56
25	57
26	58
27	59
28	60
29	61
30	62
31	63
32	64

小

京	景	寮	県	糸	系
capital city	scenery	hostel, dormitory	prefecture	thread	lineage; group
KYŌ KEI	KEI	RYŌ	KEN	SHI	KEI
#	#	#	#	ito	#
r 8　s 8	r 72　s 12	r 40　s 15	r 109*　s 9	r 120　s 6	r 120　s 7

乗	余	茶	荒
ride	remainder; surplus	tea	wild
-	-		-
JŌ	YO	CHA SA	KŌ
no*ru*..	ama*ru*..	#	ara*i* a+
r 4　s 9	r 9　s 7	r 140　s 9	r 140　s 9

原	療	斎
prairie; origin	treat illness	purify; abstain from
GEN	RYŌ	SAI
hara	#	#
r 27　s 10	r 104　s 17	r 67*　s 11

示

示	宗	票	崇
show	religion	vote; chit	venerate
-	-		-
SHI JI	SHŪ SŌ	HYŌ	SŪ
shime*su*	#	#	#
r 113　s 5	r 40　s 8	r 113　s 11	r 46　s 11

禁	祭	察
prohibit	festival	inspect; guess
-	-	
KIN	SAI	SATSU
#	matsu*ru*..	#
r 113　s 13	r 113　s 11	r 40　s 14

水

泉	暴	泰	康	尿	衆
spring; spa	violent	tranquil	healthy; safe	urine	the people
		-			-
SEN	BŌ BAKU	TAI	KŌ	NYŌ	SHŪ SHU
izumi	aba*reru*..	#	#	#	#
r 85　s 9	r 72　s 15	r 85　s 10	r 53　s 11	r 44　s 7	r 143　s 12

糸

系	素	索	累
lineage; group	basic, bare	cord; seek	accumulate
KEI	SO SU	SAKU	RUI
#	#	#	#
r 120　s 7	r 120　s 10	r 120　s 10	r 120　s 11

紫	緊	繁
purple	tight	flourishing
-	-	-
SHI	KIN	HAN
murasaki	#	#
r 120　s 12	r 120　s 15	r 120　s 16

刀　力　木

刀

分	券	雰	寡	秀
portion; minutes	ticket	atmosphere	few; widow	excellent
BU FUN BUN	KEN	FUN	KA	SHŪ
wakeru..	#	#	#	hiideru
r 18 s 4	r 18 s 8	r 173 s 12	r 40 s 14	r 115 s 7

力

労	劣	男	勇	募	努
labor	inferior	male	courage	raise funds, recruit	effort
RŌ	RETSU	DAN NAN	YŪ	BO	DO
#	otoru	otoko	isamu	tsunoru	tsutomeru
r 19 s 7	r 19 s 6	r 102 s 7	r 19 s 9	r 19 s 12	r 19 s 7

勢	虜	万	方	芳	房
power; tendency	captive	ten thousand; many	direction; side; person	fragrant; (honorific) your	room; tassel
SEI	RYO	MAN BAN	HŌ	HŌ	BŌ
Ikioi	#	#	kata	kanbashii	fusa
r 19 s 13	r 141 s 13	r 1* s 3	r 70 s 4	r 140 s 7	r 63 s 8

木

果	某	栄	菜	菓	巣
fruit, result	a certain (eg person)	glory; prosper	vegetable	candy, cake	nest
KA	BŌ	EI	SAI	KA	SŌ
hatasu..	#	hae.. saka+	na	#	su
r 75 s 8	r 75 s 9	r 75 s 9	r 140 s 11	r 140 s 11	r 75* s 11

条	柔	案	棄	集	業
clause	soft	plan	abandon	gather	business; deed, act
JŌ	JŪ NYŪ	AN	KI	SHŪ	GYŌ GŌ
#	yawaraka..	#	#	tsudou atsu+	waza
r 75 s 7	r 75 s 9	r 75 s 10	r 75 s 13	r 172 s 12	r 75 s 13

葉	薬	染	架
leaf	medicine, drug	dye	beam, frame; span (gap)
YŌ	YAKU	SEN	KA
ha	kusuri	someru.. shi+	kakeru..
r 140 s 12	r 140 s 16	r 75 s 9	r 75 s 9

楽	桑	築
music; joy	mulberry	construct, build
GAKU RAKU	SŌ	CHIKU
tanoshii..	kuwa	kizuku
r 75 s 13	r 75 s 10	r 118 s 16

床	閑	米	茶
bed; floor	leisure	rice; America	tea
SHŌ	KAN	BEI MAI	CHA SA
toko yuka	#	kome	#
r 53 s 7	r 169 s 12	r 119 s 6	r 140 s 9

1	33
2	34
3	35
4	36
5	37
6	38
7	39
8	40
9	41
10	42
11	43
12	44
13	45
14	**46**
15	47
16	48
17	49
18	50
19	51
20	52
21	53
22	54
23	55
24	56
25	57
26	58
27	59
28	60
29	61
30	62
31	63
32	64

立	豆	翌	登	豊	痘
stand, rise, set up	bean; miniature	next	climb	abundant	smallpox
RITSU RYU	TŌ ZU	-	TŌ TO	HŌ	TŌ
ta*tsu*..	mame	YOKU	nobo*ru*	yutaka	-
r 117　s 5	r 151　s 7	#	TŌ TO	yutaka	#
		r 124　s 11	r 105　s 12	r 151　s 13	r 104　s 12

並	霊	虚
line up; ordinary	spirit, soul	void
HEI	REI RYŌ	-
nara*bu*.. nami	tama	KYO KO
r 1*　s 8	r 173　s 15	#
		r 141　s 11

点	魚	無	焦	馬	鳥
point, dot	fish	without, -less; not be	scorch; hasty	horse	bird
TEN	-	MU BU	SHŌ	BA	CHŌ
#	GYO	nai	ko*gasu*.. ase+	uma ma	tori
r 86*　s 9	sakana uo	r 86　s 12	r 86　s 12	r 187　s 10	r 196　s 11
	r 195　s 11				

黒	煮	薫	蒸	窯	為
black	boil, cook	fragrant	steam; sultry	kiln	do; purpose
-	SHA	-	JŌ	-	I
KOKU	ni*eru*..	KUN	mu*su*..	YŌ	#
kuro kuro+	r 86　s 12	kao*ru*	r 140　s 13	kama	r 86*　s 9
r 203　s 11		r 140　s 16		r 116　s 15	

烈	照	然	黙
intense	shine; embarrassed	-like; nature	silent
-	SHŌ	ZEN NEN	-
RETSU	te*ru*..	#	MOKU
#	r 86　s 13	r 86　s 12	dama*ru*
r 86　s 10			r 203　s 15

勲	熱	熟	庶	薦
meritorious	heat; fever	mature	multitude	recommend
-	NETSU	-	SHO	SEN
KUN	atsu*i*	JUKU	#	susu*meru*
#	r 86　s 15	u*reru*	r 53　s 11	r 140　s 16
r 19　s 15		r 86　s 15		

恭	慕
respect	adore; yearn
-	BO
KYŌ	shita*u*
uyauya*shii*	r 61　s 14
r 61　s 10	

忌 mourn; abhor KI imu.. r61 s7	忠 loyalty CHŪ # r61 s8	患 ill KAN wazurau r61 s11	忍 endure; conceal NIN shinobu.. r61 s7	志 aspire, intend SHI kokorozashi kokoroza+ r61 s7	
忘 forget - BŌ wasureru r61 s7	恋 romantic love REN koi ko+ koi+ r61 s10	思 think - SHI omou r61 s9	恩 grace; favor ON # r61 s10	悪 bad, wicked AKU O warui r61 s11	恵 favor, kindness KEI E megumu r61 s10
忘 forget - BŌ wasureru r61 s7	恋 romantic love REN koi ko+ koi+ r61 s10	急 hurry; sudden KYŪ isogu r61 s9	念 thought; desire NEN # r61 s9	息 breath; child SOKU iki r61 s10	怠 lazy; neglect TAI okotaru nama+ r61 s9
愚 foolish - GU oroka r61 s13	意 intent; mind I # r61 s13	窓 window - SŌ mado r116 s11	憲 the law, constitution KEN # r61 s16	慈 compassion - JI itsukushimu r61 s13	
悲 sad - HI kanashii.. r61 s12	恐 fear - KYŌ osoreru.. r61 s10	怒 anger - DO okoru ika+ r61 s9	想 thought SŌ SO # r61 s13	愁 sorrow - SHŪ urei.. r61 s13	悠 relax - KEI ikoi.. r61 s16
憩 relaxed; far YŪ # r61 s11	懸 hang; risk KEN KE kakaru.. r61 s20	慰 console, cheer up I nagusameru r61 s15	懇 intimate; kind; polite; sincere KON nengoro r61 s17	態 appearance; state, condition TAI # r61 s14	懲 punish, chastise CHŌ korasu.. r61 s18
惑 astray; mislead WAKU madou r61 s12	感 senses; feel KAN # r61 s13	恩 grace; favor ON # r61 s10	思 think - SHI omou r61 s9		
応 respond - Ō # r61 s7	慮 consider; concern for RYO # r61 s15	癒 heal - YU # r104 s18			

1	33
2	34
3	35
4	36
5	37
6	38
7	39
8	40
9	41
10	42
11	43
12	44
13	45
14	46
15	**47**
16	48
17	49
18	50
19	51
20	52
21	53
22	54
23	55
24	56
25	57
26	58
27	59
28	60
29	61
30	62
31	63
32	64

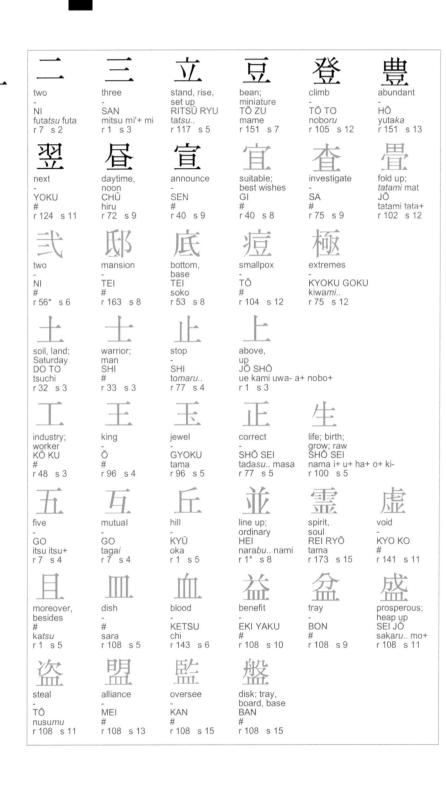

一

二 two - NI futa*tsu* futa r 7 s 2	三 three - SAN mitsu mi'+ mi r 1 s 3	立 stand, rise, set up RITSU RYU ta*tsu*.. r 117 s 5	豆 bean; miniature TŌ ZU mame r 151 s 7	登 climb - TŌ TO nobo*ru* r 105 s 12	豊 abundant - HŌ yuta*ka* r 151 s 13
翌 next YOKU # r 124 s 11	昼 daytime, noon CHŪ hiru r 72 s 9	宣 announce - SEN # r 40 s 9	宜 suitable; best wishes GI # r 40 s 8	査 investigate - SA # r 75 s 9	畳 fold up; *tatami* mat JŌ tatami tata+ r 102 s 12
弐 two - NI # r 56* s 6	邸 mansion TEI # r 163 s 8	底 bottom, base TEI soko r 53 s 8	痘 smallpox TŌ # r 104 s 12	極 extremes KYOKU GOKU kiwa*mi*.. r 75 s 12	
土 soil, land; Saturday DO TO tsuchi r 32 s 3	士 warrior; man SHI # r 33 s 3	止 stop - SHI to*maru*.. r 77 s 4	上 above, up JŌ SHŌ ue kami uwa- a+ nobo+ r 1 s 3		
工 industry; worker KŌ KU # r 48 s 3	王 king - Ō # r 96 s 4	玉 jewel - GYOKU tama r 96 s 5	正 correct - SHŌ SEI tada*su*.. masa r 77 s 5	生 life; birth; grow; raw SHŌ SEI nama i+ u+ ha+ o+ ki- r 100 s 5	
五 five - GO itsu itsu+ r 7 s 4	互 mutual - GO taga*i* r 7 s 4	丘 hill - KYŪ oka r 1 s 5	並 line up; ordinary HEI nara*bu*.. nami r 1* s 8	霊 spirit, soul REI RYŌ tama r 173 s 15	虚 void - KYO KO # r 141 s 11
且 moreover, besides # ka*tsu* r 1 s 5	皿 dish - # sara r 108 s 5	血 blood - KETSU chi r 143 s 6	益 benefit - EKI YAKU # r 108 s 10	盆 tray - BON # r 108 s 9	盛 prosperous; heap up SEI JŌ saka*ru*.. mo+ r 108 s 11
盗 steal - TŌ nusu*mu* r 108 s 11	盟 alliance - MEI # r 108 s 13	監 oversee - KAN # r 108 s 15	盤 disk; tray, board, base BAN # r 108 s 15		

⬛ 山 土 止

山

出 go out, exit; put out; SHUTSU SUI; de*ru* da+; r 17 s 5

缶 tin can; -; KAN; #; r 121 s 6

岳 mountain peak; GAKU; take; r 46 s 8

両 both; -; RYŌ; #; r 1* s 6

密 secret; dense; delicate; MITSU; #; r 40 s 11

屈 bend; yield; KUTSU; #; r 44 s 8

島 island; -; TŌ; shima; r 46 s 10

幽 deep; hidden; remote; …; YŪ; #; r 52 s 9

土

里 village; ri; RI; sato; r 166 s 7

堂 hall; temple; DŌ; #; r 32 s 11

至 arrive; utmost; SHI; ita*ru*; r 133 s 6

室 room; -; SHITSU; muro; r 40 s 9

窒 suffocate; plug; CHITSU; #; r 116 s 11

重 heavy; layered; JŪ CHŌ; omo*i* kasa+ -e; r 166 s 9

茎 stalk, stem; KEI; kuki; r 140 s 8

墓 grave, tomb; BO; haka; r 32 s 13

基 foundations; -; KI; moto motoi; r 32 s 11

塁 fort; base (baseball); RUI; #; r 32 s 12

墨 India ink; BOKU; sumi; r 32 s 14

型 template; -; KEI; kata; r 32 s 9

堅 firm, hard; KEN; kata*i*; r 32 s 12

塗 paint; -; TO; nu*ru*; r 32 s 13

墜 fall, drop; TSUI; #; r 32 s 15

堕 degenerate; -; DA; #; r 32 s 12

塑 model, molding; SO; #; r 32 s 13

墾 clear land, cultivate; KON; #; r 32 s 16

壁 wall; -; HEKI; kabe; r 32 s 16

塾 cram school; JUKU; #; r 32 s 14

圧 pressure; -; ATSU; #; r 32 s 5

在 be located; exist; suburbs; ZAI; a*ru*; r 32 s 6

座 sit, seat; ZA; suwa*ru*; r 53 s 10

屋 house; -seller; OKU; ya; r 44 s 9

厘 *rin*; -; RIN; #; r 27 s 9

童 child; -; DŌ; warabe; r 117 s 12

量 quantity; -; RYŌ; haka*ru*; r 166 s 12

止

企 plan; -; KI; kuwada*teru*; r 9 s 6

整 arrange; -; SEI; totono*eru*..; r 66 s 16

武 military; -; BU MU; #; r 77 s 8

歴 history, career, CV.; -; REKI; #; r 77 s 14

症 symptoms; -; SHŌ; #; r 104 s 10

1	33
2	34
3	35
4	36
5	37
6	38
7	39
8	40
9	41
10	42
11	43
12	44
13	45
14	46
15	47
16	**48**
17	49
18	50
19	51
20	52
21	53
22	54
23	55
24	56
25	57
26	58
27	59
28	60
29	61
30	62
31	63
32	64

乂

文	父	交
literature	father	intercourse
-	-	-
BUN MON	FU	KŌ
fumi	chichi	ma*jiru* maji+ ka+
r 67 s 4	r 88 s 4	r 8 s 6

気	茂	及	匁
spirit; air	luxuriant, overgrown	attain	*monme*
		-	-
KI KE	MO	KYŪ	#
#	shige*ru*	oyo*bu*..	monme
r 84 s 6	r 140 s 8	r 29 s 3	r 20 s 4

又

支	受	隻	反	友	皮
branch; support	receive	one (of a pair)	oppose; bend, warp	friend	skin
SHI	JU	SEKI	HAN HON TAN	YŪ	HI
sasa*eru*	u*keru*..	#	so*ru*..	tomo	kawa
r 65 s 4	r 29 s 8	r 172 s 10	r 29 s 4	r 29 s 4	r 107 s 5

度	疫	疲	髪
degree, extent; times; …	epidemic	fatigue	hair
DO TAKU TO	-	-	-
tabi	EKI YAKU	HI	HATSU
	#	tsuka*reru*..	kami
r 53 s 9	r 104 s 9	r 104 s 10	r 190 s 14

夂

麦	変	夏	憂	愛	慶
cereal	alter; odd	summer	anxiety; sorrow	love	celebrate
-		-		-	-
BAKU	HEN	KA GE	YŪ	AI	KEI
mugi	kawa*ru*..	natsu	ure*eru*.. u+	#	#
r 199 s 7	r 34* s 9	r 34* s 10	r 61 s 15	r 61 s 13	r 61 s 15

女

安	妄	妥	委	要
calm; cheap	reckless	agree; calm	entrust	essential
AN	-	DA	-	-
yasu*i*	MŌ BŌ	#	I	YŌ
	#		#	i*ru*
r 40 s 6	r 38 s 6	r 38 s 7	r 38 s 8	r 146 s 9

宴	妻	姿	婆
banquet	wife	figure	old woman
-			-
EN	SAI	SHI	BA
#	tsuma	sugata	#
r 40 s 10	r 38 s 8	r 38 s 9	r 38 s 11

止	
火 大 工 王	

止

走 run - SŌ hashir*u* r 156 s 7

足 foot, leg; suffice SOKU ashi ta+ r 157 s 7

是 right, just; this ZE # r 72 s 9

定 fix, decide TEI JŌ sada*meru*.. r 40 s 8

火

災 disaster - SAI wazawa*i* r 86 s 7

炎 inflame - EN honō r 86 s 8

灰 ash - KAI hai r 86 s 6

炭 charcoal - TAN sumi r 86 s 9

大

突 thrust - TOTSU tsu*ku* r 116 s 8

臭 stinking - SHŪ kusa*i* r 132 s 9

奥 inmost, core Ō oku r 37 s 12

奨 encourage - SHŌ # r 37 s 13

契 pledge - KEI chigi*ru* r 37 s 9

喫 eat, drink, smoke KITSU # r 30 s 12

天 heaven, sky TEN ame ama- r 37 s 4

矢 arrow - SHI ya r 111 s 5

笑 laugh - SHŌ wara*u* e+ r 118 s 10

奏 play music - SŌ kana*deru* r 37 s 9

美 beauty - BI utsuku*shii* r 123 s 9

戻 return - REI modo*ru*.. r 63 s 7

工

空 air, sky; empty KŪ sora a+ kara r 116 s 8

式 rite; style SHIKI # r 56 s 6

左 left (hand) SA hidari r 48 s 5

差 difference - SA sa*su* r 48 s 10

王

主 master - SHU SU nushi omo r 3 s 5

全 whole - ZEN matta*ku* r 9* s 6

呈 presentation - TEI # r 30 s 8

皇 emperor - Ō KŌ # r 106 s 9

望 hope; view BŌ MŌ nozo*mu* r 130* s 11

聖 holy - SEI # r 128 s 13

星 star - SEI SHŌ hoshi r 72 s 9

産 give birth - SAN ubu u+ r 100 s 11

宝 treasure - HŌ takara r 40 s 8

璽 imperial seal - JI # r 96 s 19

囗　丁　于　子　手

丁	予	亭	寧		
	pre-, fore-;	inn	calm		
	I	-	-		
	YO	TEI	NEI		
	#	#	#		
	r 6* s 4	r 8 s 9	r 40 s 14		
	庁	序	斤	子	
	government	preface;	*kin*	child	
	agency	rank, order	-	-	
	CHŌ	JO	KIN	SHI SU	
	#	#	#	ko	
	r 53 s 5	r 53 s 7	r 69 s 4	r 39 s 3	

于	宇	芋	辛	宰	幸
	cosmos	potato	spicy;	supervise,	happiness,
	-	-	hardship	manage	good fortune
	U	#	SHIN	SAI	KŌ
	#	imo	kara*i*	#	saiw*ai* shiawa+ sachi
	r 40 s 6	r 140 s 6	r 160 s 7	r 40 s 10	r 51 s 8
	岸	南			
	shore	south			
	-	-			
	GAN	NAN NA			
	kishi	minami			
	r 46 s 8	r 24 s 9			

子	字	学	享	季	孝
	character,	study,	enjoy;	season	filial
	kanji, word	learning	receive	-	piety
	JI	GAKU	KYŌ	KI	KŌ
	aza	mana*bu*	#	#	#
	r 39 s 6	r 39 s 8	r 8 s 8	r 39 s 8	r 39 s 7
	存	厚			
	exist;	thick;			
	think that	cordial			
	SON ZON	KŌ			
	#	atsu*i*			
	r 39 s 6	r 27 s 9			

手	挙	掌	撃	摩	
	raise; arrest;	control;	strike,	rub	
	whole; …	palm (of hand)	attack	-	
	KYO	SHŌ	GEKI	MA	
	a*geru*..	#	u*tsu*	#	
	r 64 s 10	r 64 s 12	r 64 s 15	r 64 s 15	

ム 云 𧘇 衣 𧘇

ム

公 public; official — KŌ — ōyake — r 12 s 4

玄 dark; occult — GEN — # — r 95 s 5

去 depart; past, gone — KYO KO — saru — r 28 s 5

広 wide — - — KŌ — hiroi.. — r 53 s 5

云

会 meet — - — KAI E — au — r 9* s 6

芸 art, skill — - — GEI — # — r 140 s 7

雲 cloud — - — UN — kumo — r 173 s 12

曇 cloudy — - — DON — kumoru — r 72 s 16

𧘇

衣 garment — - — I — koromo — r 145 s 6

衰 decline — - — SUI — otoroeru — r 145 s 10

衷 inmost — - — CHŪ — # — r 2* s 9

哀 pity, grief — AI — aware.. — r 30 s 9

表 surface; chart; display — HYŌ — omote arawa+ — r 145 s 8

裏 back, rear — RI — ura — r 145 s 13

褒 praise — - — HŌ — homeru — r 145 s 15

衣

袋 bag — - — TAI — fukuro — r 145 s 11

装 put on, wear; equip — SŌ SHŌ — yosōu — r 145 s 12

裂 split — - — RETSU — sakeru.. — r 145 s 12

製 manufacture — - — SEI — # — r 145 s 14

襲 raid; inherit — SHŪ — osou — r 145 s 22

裁 judge; cut — SAI — sabaku ta+ — r 145 s 12

𧘇

長 long; chief — CHŌ — nagai — r 168 s 8

喪 mourning — - — SŌ — mo — r 30 s 12

展 display, unfold — TEN — # — r 44 s 10

農 farming — - — NŌ — # — r 161 s 13

震 quake — - — SHIN — furueru.. — r 173 s 15

養 foster, rear — YŌ — yashinau — r 184 s 15

1	33
2	34
3	35
4	36
5	37
6	38
7	39
8	40
9	41
10	42
11	43
12	44
13	45
14	46
15	47
16	48
17	49
18	**50**
19	51
20	52
21	53
22	54
23	55
24	56
25	57
26	58
27	59
28	60
29	61
30	62
31	63
32	64

占
divination;
occupy
SEN
uran*au* shi+
r 25 s 5

古
old,
antiquated
KO
furu*i..*
r 30 s 5

舌
tongue
-
ZETSU
shita
r 135 s 6

否
negate
-
HI
ina
r 30 s 7

吉
lucky
-
KICHI KITSU
#
r 30 s 6

告
notify,
announce
KOKU
tsu*geru*
r 30 s 7

合
unite;
agree; fit
GŌ GA' KA'
a*u..*
r 30 s 6

谷
valley
-
KOKU
tani
r 150 s 7

舍
building,
house, hut
SHA
#
r 9* s 8

含
include,
contain
GAN
fuku*mu..*
r 30 s 7

台
pedestal;
Taiwan
DAI TAI
#
r 30* s 5

名
name;
fame
MEI MYŌ
na
r 30 s 6

各
each
-
KAKU
onoono
r 30 s 6

召
summon
-
SHŌ
me*su*
r 30 s 5

君
lord;
you
KUN
kimi
r 30 s 7

害
harm
-
GAI
#
r 40 s 10

容
looks;
contain
YŌ
#
r 40 s 10

客
guest,
customer
KYAKU KAKU
#
r 40 s 9

答
answer
-
TŌ
kotae..
r 118 s 12

苦
pain;
bitter
KU
kuru*shii..* niga+
r 140 s 8

宮
shrine,
palace
KYŪ GŪ KU
miya
r 40 s 10

営
management
-
EI
itona*mu*
r 30* s 12

善
good
-
ZEN
yo*i*
r 30 s 12

喜
rejoice
-
KI
yoroko*bu*
r 30 s 12

啓
enlighten
-
KEI
#
r 30 s 11

哲
wisdom;
philosophy
TETSU
#
r 30 s 10

言
say, speak;
word
GEN GON
i*u* koto
r 149 s 7

誉
honor
-
YO
homa*re*
r 149 s 13

誓
vow
-
SEI
chika*u*
r 149 s 14

警
warn;
police
KEI
#
r 149 s 19

□

□

右	stone	

右
right (hand)
-
U YŪ
migi
r 30 s 5

石
stone
-
SEKI SHAKU
ishi
r 112 s 5

后
empress
-
KŌ
#
r 30 s 6

店
shop, store
-
TEN
mise
r 53 s 8

唐
Cathay; *Tang*
-
TŌ
Kara
r 30 s 10

若
young
-
JAKU NYAKU
waka*i* mo+
r 140 s 8

岩
rock, boulder
-
GAN
iwa
r 46 s 8

碁
go (the board game)
-
GO
#
r 112 s 13

磨
polish
-
MA
miga*ku*
r 112 s 16

局
bureau; local; state, condition
KYOKU
#
r 44 s 7

唇
lips
-
SHIN
kuchibiru
r 30 s 10

居
reside, be present
-
KYO
i*ru*
r 44 s 8

倉
warehouse
-
SŌ
kura
r 9 s 10

可
possible; approve
KA
#
r 30 s 5

司
official; officiate
SHI
#
r 30 s 5

句
phrase
-
KU
#
r 30 s 5

奇
strange
-
KI
#
r 37 s 8

寄
approach; give
KI
yo*ru*..
r 40 s 11

尚
facing
-
KŌ
mu*kau*..
r 30 s 6

向
respect; valued
SHŌ
#
r 42 s 8

同
same
-
DŌ
ona*ji*
r 30 s 6

周
circum-ference
SHŪ
mawa*ri*
r 30 s 8

問
question
-
MON
to*i*.. ton
r 30 s 11

閣
tower; cabinet
KAKU
#
r 169 s 14

高
high, tall; sum
KŌ
taka taka+
r 189 s 10

宮
shrine, palace
KYŪ GŪ KU
miya
r 40 s 10

官
official; government
KAN
#
r 40 s 8

管
pipe; control
KAN
kuda
r 118 s 14

筒
tube
-
TŌ
tsutsu
r 118 s 12

荷
load, cargo
KA
ni
r 140 s 10

1	33
2	34
3	35
4	36
5	37
6	38
7	39
8	40
9	41
10	42
11	43
12	44
13	45
14	46
15	47
16	48
17	49
18	50
19	**51**
20	52
21	53
22	54
23	55
24	56
25	57
26	58
27	59
28	60
29	61
30	62
31	63
32	64

日

旨	香	音	昔	普	曹
gist	fragrance	sound	ancient	universal	lawyer; companion
-	-	-	-	-	-
SHI	KŌ KYŌ	ON IN	SEKI SHAKU	FU	SŌ
mune	ka kao+	oto ne	mukashi	#	#
r 72　s 6	r 186　s 9	r 180　s 9	r 72　s 8	r 72　s 12	r 72*　s 11

書	春	百	白		
write; book	springtime	hundred	white		
SHO	SHUN	HYAKU	HAKU BYAKU		
ka*ku*	haru	#	shir*oi* shiro shira-		
r 72*　s 10	r 72　s 9	r 106　s 6	r 106　s 5		

者	署	暑	暮	著	
person	signature; (police) station	hot weather, summer	live; end; dusk	author; notable	
-					
SHA	SHO	SHO	BO	CHO	
mono	#	atsu*i*	ku*reru..*	arawa*su* ichijiru+	
r 125　s 8	r 122　s 13	r 72　s 12	r 72　s 14	r 140　s 11	

皆	習	替	暫	響	
all	learn	exchange	temporary	echo	
-	-	-	-	-	
KAI	SHŪ	TAI	ZAN	KYŌ	
mina	nara*u*	ka*eru..*	#	hibi*ku*	
r 106　s 9	r 124　s 11	r 72*　s 12	r 72　s 15	r 180　s 20	

旬	暦	間	簡	層	
10 day period	calendar	interval	simple, brief	layer	
JUN SHUN	- REKI	- KAN KEN	KAN	- SŌ	
#	koyomi	aida ma	#	#	
r 72　s 6	r 72　s 14	r 169　s 12	r 118　s 18	r 44　s 14	

白

皆	習	百
all	learn	hundred
-	-	-
KAI	SHŪ	HYAKU
mina	nara*u*	#
r 106　s 9	r 124　s 11	r 106　s 6

月

肖	育	肯	青	宵	背
resemble	bring up (child)	agreement	blue, green; young	dusk	back, rear; stature; defy
-	IKU	-	SEI SHŌ	-	HAI
SHŌ	soda*teru..*	KŌ	ao ao+	SHŌ	se sei somo+
#		#		yoi	
r 130　s 7	r 130　s 8	r 130　s 8	r 174　s 8	r 40　s 10	r 130　s 9

胃	骨	脅	有	肩	膚
stomach	bone	threaten	have; exist	shoulder	skin
-	-	-	YŪ U	-	-
I	KOTSU	KYŌ	aru	KEN	FU
#	hone	obiya*kasu* odo+		kata	#
r 130　s 9	r 188　s 10	r 130　s 10	r 130*　s 6	r 130　s 8	r 130　s 15

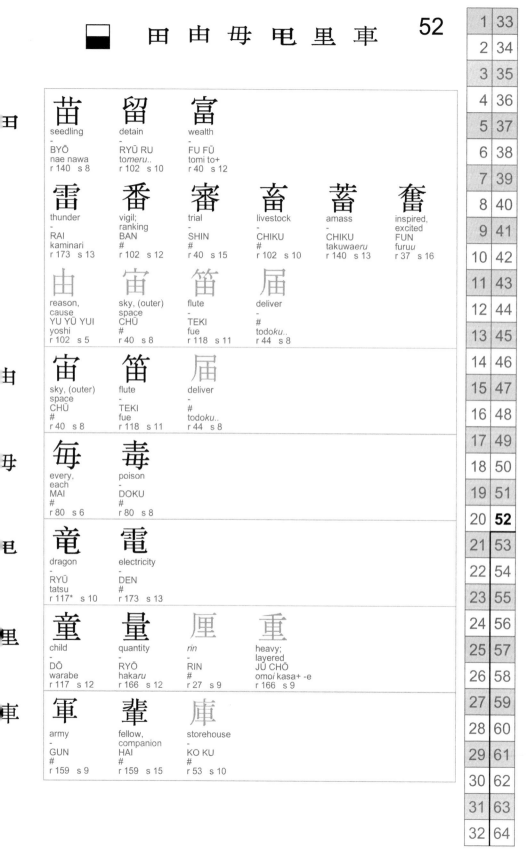

田

苗	留	富
seedling	detain	wealth
-	-	-
BYŌ	RYŪ RU	FU FŪ
nae nawa	to*meru*..	tomi to+
r 140 s 8	r 102 s 10	r 40 s 12

雷	番	審	畜	蓄	奮
thunder	vigil; ranking	trial	livestock	amass	inspired, excited
-	BAN	-	-	-	FUN
RAI	#	SHIN	CHIKU	CHIKU	furu*u*
kaminari		#	#	takuwa*eru*	
r 173 s 13	r 102 s 12	r 40 s 15	r 102 s 10	r 140 s 13	r 37 s 16

由	宙	笛	届
reason, cause	sky, (outer) space	flute	deliver
YU YŪ YUI	CHŪ	TEKI	#
yoshi	#	fue	todo*ku*..
r 102 s 5	r 40 s 8	r 118 s 11	r 44 s 8

由

宙	笛	届
sky, (outer) space	flute	deliver
CHŪ	-	-
#	TEKI	#
	fue	todo*ku*..
r 40 s 8	r 118 s 11	r 44 s 8

母

毎	毒
every, each	poison
MAI	-
#	DOKU
	#
r 80 s 6	r 80 s 8

甩

竜	電
dragon	electricity
-	-
RYŪ	DEN
tatsu	#
r 117* s 10	r 173 s 13

里

童	量	厘	重
child	quantity	*rin*	heavy; layered
-	-	-	JŪ CHŌ
DŌ	RYŌ	RIN	omo*i* kasa+ -e
warabe	haka*ru*	#	
r 117 s 12	r 166 s 12	r 27 s 9	r 166 s 9

車

軍	輩	庫
army	fellow, companion	storehouse
-	-	-
GUN	HAI	KO KU
#	#	#
r 159 s 9	r 159 s 15	r 53 s 10

目

首	盲	冒	省
head, neck; chief	blind	risk; defy	minister; omit; reflect upon; …
SHU	MŌ	BŌ	SHŌ SEI
kubi	#	okasu	habuku kaeri+
r 185　s 9	r 109　s 8	r 109*　s 9	r 109　s 9

督	看	着	盾	自
supervise	watch over	arrive; wear, clothes	shield	oneself
-				
TOKU	KAN	CHAKU JAKU	JUN	JI SHI
#	#	kiru.. tsu+	tate	mizukara
r 109　s 13	r 109　s 9	r 109*　s 12	r 109　s 9	r 132　s 6

且

宜	査	畳
suitable; best wishes	investigate	fold up; *tatami* mat
GI	SA	JŌ
#	#	tatami tata+
r 40　s 8	r 75　s 9	r 102　s 12

貝

貞	負	貢	員	買
chastity	defeated; bear, suffer	tribute	member	buy
-		-	-	-
TEI	FU	KŌ KU	IN	BAI
#	makeru.. o+	mitsugu	#	kau
r 154　s 9	r 154　s 9	r 154　s 10	r 30　s 10	r 154　s 12

貴	貫	責	費	賞	賓
noble, valued	pierce; carry through	blame; duty	cost	prize	guest
KI	KAN	SEKI	HI	SHŌ	HIN
tattoi.. tōto+	tsuranuku	semeru	tsuiyasu..	#	#
r 154　s 12	r 154　s 11	r 154　s 11	r 154　s 12	r 154　s 15	r 154　s 15

貧	貨	貸	賃	資
poverty	goods; coin, money	lend, rent out	fee, wages	assets
-				-
HIN BIN	KA	TAI	CHIN	SHI
mazushii	#	kasu	#	#
r 154　s 11	r 154　s 11	r 154　s 12	r 154　s 13	r 154　s 13

賛	賀	貿	賢	質
praise, approve	good wishes	trade	wise	quality; hostage
SAN	GA	BŌ	KEN	SHITSU SHICHI CHI
#	#	#	kashikoi	#
r 154　s 15	r 154　s 12	r 154　s 12	r 154　s 16	r 154　s 15

見

覚	寛	覧
memorize; awake	tolerant	look at
KAKU	KAN	RAN
oboeru sa+	#	#
r 147　s 12	r 40　s 13	r 147　s 17

石 皿 吅 虫 言

石

岩	碁	磨	若
rock, boulder	go (the board game)	polish	young
GAN	GO	MA	JAKU NYAKU
iwa	#	migaku	wakai mo+
r 46 s 8	r 112 s 13	r 112 s 16	r 140 s 8

皿

益	盆	盛	血
benefit	tray	prosperous; heap up	blood
-	-	-	-
EKI YAKU	BON	SEI JŌ	KETSU
#	#	sakaru.. mo+	chi
r 108 s 10	r 108 s 9	r 108 s 11	r 143 s 6

盗	盟	監	盤
steal	alliance	oversee	disk; tray, board, base
-	-	-	-
TŌ	MEI	KAN	BAN
nusumu	#	#	#
r 108 s 11	r 108 s 13	r 108 s 15	r 108 s 15

吅

器
container; utensil; skill
KI
utsuwa
r 30 s 15

語	詔	話	詰	諾	諮
language, word; talk	imperial edict	speak; tale	cram; rebuke	consent	consult
GO	SHŌ	WA	KITSU	-	-
kataru..	mikotonori	hanashi hana+	tsumu..	DAKU	SHI
r 149 s 14	r 149 s 12	r 149 s 13	r 149 s 13	#	hakaru
				r 149 s 15	r 149 s 16

虫

蛍	蛮	蚕	風
firefly	barbarian	silkworm	wind; style
-	-	-	
KEI	BAN	SAN	FŪ FU
hotaru	#	kaiko	kaze kaza-
r 142 s 11	r 142 s 12	r 142 s 10	r 182 s 9

言

誉	誓	警
honor	vow	warn; police
-	-	-
YO	SEI	KEI
homare	chikau	#
r 149 s 13	r 149 s 14	r 149 s 19

	策	筆	奔	星	産
朿 聿 丹 生	plan, policy SAKU # r 118 s 12	writing brush HITSU fude r 118 s 12	hurry - HON # r 37 s 8	star - SEI SHŌ hoshi r 72 s 9	give birth - SAN ubu u+ r 100 s 11
	亡	奉	半	暴	泰
乚 キ 氺	deceased - BŌ MŌ nai r 8 s 3	offering; respectful HŌ BU tatematsuru r 37 s 8	half, semi-, pen- HAN nakaba r 24 s 5	violent - BŌ BAKU abareru.. r 72 s 15	tranquil - TAI # r 85 s 10
	芝	翌	歩	養	
之 立 少 良	turf # shiba r 140 s 6	next - YOKU # r 124 s 11	walk - HO BU FU aruku ayu+ r 77 s 8	foster, rear YŌ yashinau r 184 s 15	
	斉	斎	粛	肉	腐
月 尸 刪 人	equal - SEI # r 67* s 8	purify; abstain from SAI # r 67* s 11	solemn; purge SHUKU # r 129 s 11	meat, flesh - NIKU # r 130 s 6	rot - FU kusaru.. r 130 s 14
	究	卑	髪	芳	房
九 午 友 方	research, investigate KYŪ kiwameru r 116 s 7	lowly - HI iyashii.. r 24 s 9	hair - HATSU kami r 190 s 14	fragrant; (honorific) your HŌ kanbashii r 140 s 7	room; tassel BŌ fusa r 63 s 8
	多	夢	易	参	
夕 勿 乡	many - TA ōi r 36 s 6	dream - MU yume r 36 s 13	easy; trade; divination EKI I yasashii r 72 s 8	visit; join in SAN mairu r 28 s 8	
	考	昇	義	養	
ㄅ 升 我 食	consider - KŌ kangaeru r 125 s 6	rise - SHŌ noboru r 72 s 8	righteous; meaning; ... GI # r 123 s 13	foster, rear YŌ yashinau r 184 s 15	
	界	琴	零	雰	
介 今 令 分	world; scope KAI # r 102 s 9	harp - KIN koto r 96 s 12	zero - REI # r 173 s 13	atmosphere - FUN # r 173 s 12	

◨

万 而 才 无

亜 正

玉 豆

疋 夭 毛

彐 了 乃

卂 弟 巳

已 艮 彐

四 辰 馬

号	需	矛	発	
number, designation	need, demand	spear, lance	emit; start	
GŌ	JU	MU	HATSU HOTSU	
#	#	hoko	#	
r 30* s 5	r 173 s 14	r 110 s 5	r 105 s 9	

並	霊	整	症	
line up; ordinary	spirit, soul	arrange	symptoms	
HEI	REI RYŌ	SEI	SHŌ	
narabu.. nami	tama	sadameru..	#	
r 1* s 8	r 173 s 15	r 66 s 16	r 104 s 10	

宝	璽	登	豊	痘
treasure	imperial seal	climb	abundant	smallpox
HŌ	JI	TŌ TO	HŌ	TŌ
takara	#	noboru	yutaka	#
r 40 s 8	r 96 s 19	r 105 s 12	r 151 s 13	r 104 s 12

定	是	奏	笑	宅
fix, decide	right, just; this	play music	laugh	home
TEI JŌ	ZE	SŌ	SHŌ	TAKU
totonoeru..	#	kanaderu..	warau e+	#
r 40 s 8	r 72 s 9	r 37 s 9	r 118 s 10	r 40 s 6

当	雪	今	琴	秀
hit; this; applicable	snow	now	harp	excellent
TŌ	SETSU	KIN KON	KIN	SHŪ
ateru..	yuki	ima	koto	hiideru
r 58* s 6	r 173 s 11	r 9 s 4	r 96 s 12	r 115 s 7

令	零	第	厄	危
orders	zero	Number (as in 'Number 3')	misfortune	dangerous
REI	REI	DAI	YAKU	KI
#	#	#	#	abunai aya+
r 9 s 5	r 173 s 13	r 118 s 11	r 27 s 4	r 26 s 6

巻	包	官	管	虐
roll; scroll; book	wrap	official; government	pipe; control	cruel
KAN	HŌ	KAN	KAN	GYAKU
maki ma+	tsutsumu	#	kuda	shiitageru
r 49* s 9	r 20 s 5	r 40 s 8	r 118 s 14	r 141 s 9

甚	農	震	篤	驚
extremely	farming	quake	good; seriously	surprise
JIN	NŌ	SHIN	TOKU	KYŌ
hanahada..	#	furueru..	#	odoroku..
r 99 s 9	r 161 s 13	r 173 s 15	r 118 s 16	r 187 s 22

1	33
2	34
3	35
4	36
5	37
6	38
7	39
8	40
9	41
10	42
11	43
12	44
13	45
14	46
15	47
16	48
17	49
18	50
19	51
20	52
21	53
22	**54**
23	55
24	56
25	57
26	58
27	59
28	60
29	61
30	62
31	63
32	64

□ 厂 厂 ナ ナ

厂

圧	反	厄	灰	原	厚
pressure	oppose; bend, warp	misfortune	ash	prairie; origin	thick; cordial
-	HAN HON TAN	-	-	GEN	KŌ
ATSU	so*ru*..	YAKU	KAI	hara	atsu*i*
#		#	hai		
r 32 s 5	r 29 s 4	r 27 s 4	r 86 s 6	r 27 s 10	r 27 s 9

厘	暦	歴	唇	辱	
rin	calendar	history, career, CV.	lips	disgrace, insult	
-	-	REKI	-	JOKU	
RIN	REKI	#	SHIN	hazukashi*meru*	
#	koyomi		kuchibiru		
r 27 s 9	r 72 s 14	r 77 s 14	r 30 s 10	r 161 s 10	

励	石
encourage; diligent	stone
REI	-
hage*mu*..	SEKI SHAKU
	ishi
r 19 s 7	r 112 s 5

厂

斤	斥	后	盾	丘	氏
kin	repel	empress	shield	hill	family name
-	-	-	-	KYŪ	SHI
KIN	SEKI	KŌ	JUN	oka	uji
#	#	#	tate		
r 69 s 4	r 69 s 5	r 30 s 6	r 109 s 9	r 1 s 5	r 83 s 4

ナ

左	右	友	布	有	石
left (hand)	right (hand)	friend	cloth; spread	have; exist	stone
SA	U YŪ	-	FU	YŪ U	-
hidari	migi	YŪ	nuno	*aru*	SEKI SHAKU
		tomo			ishi
r 48 s 5	r 30 s 5	r 29 s 4	r 50 s 5	r 130* s 6	r 112 s 5

ナ

在	存
be located; exist; suburbs	exist; think that
ZAI	SON ZON
aru	#
r 32 s 6	r 39 s 6

■ 广 疒 虍

庁	広	床	応	店	序
government agency	wide	bed; floor	respond	shop, store	preface; rank, order
CHŌ	- KŌ	SHŌ	- Ō	TEN	JO
#	hiro*i..*	toko yuka	#	mise	#
r 53 s 5	r 53 s 5	r 53 s 7	r 61 s 7	r 53 s 8	r 53 s 7

底	座	庶	度	席	唐
bottom, base	sit, seat	multitude	degree, extent; times; …	seat, place	Cathay; *Tang*
TEI	ZA	- SHO	DO TAKU TO	SEKI	TŌ
soko	suwa*ru*	#	tabi	#	Kara
r 53 s 8	r 53 s 10	r 53 s 11	r 53 s 9	r 50 s 10	r 30 s 10

庫	廉	康	庸	皮	
storehouse	honest; cheap	healthy; safe	ordinary	skin	
- KO KU	REN	- KŌ	- YŌ	- HI	
#	#	#	#	kawa	
r 53 s 10	r 53 s 13	r 53 s 11	r 53 s 11	r 107 s 5	

府	麻	廊	庭	応	
metropolis; government	hemp; numb	corridor	garden	respond	
FU	MA	- RŌ	- TEI	- Ō	
#	asa	#	niwa	#	
r 53 s 8	r 200 s 11	r 53 s 12	r 53 s 10	r 61 s 7	

廃	磨	摩	魔	腐	慶
obsolete, waste, scrap	polish	rub	demon, devil	rot	celebrate
HAI	- MA	- MA	- MA	- FU	- KEI
sutare*ru..*	miga*ku*	#	#	kusa*ru..*	#
r 53 s 12	r 112 s 16	r 64 s 15	r 194 s 21	r 130 s 14	r 61 s 15

症	疾	疲	病	疫	痘
symptoms	disease; speed	fatigue	illness	epidemic	smallpox
- SHŌ	SHITSU	- HI	- BYŌ HEI	- EKI YAKU	- TŌ
#	#	tsuka*reru..*	yamai ya+	#	#
r 104 s 10	r 104 s 10	r 104 s 10	r 104 s 10	r 104 s 9	r 104 s 12

痛	痢	痴	癖	癒	療
pain	diarrhea	foolish	habit	heal	treat illness
- TSŪ	- RI	- CHI	- HEKI	- YU	- RYŌ
ita*mu..*	#	#	kuse	iya+ ie+	#
r 104 s 12	r 104 s 12	r 104 s 13	r 104 s 18	r 104 s 18	r 104 s 17

虐	虚	慮	虜	虞	膚
cruel	void	consider; concern for	captive	anxiety	skin
GYAKU	KYO KO	RYO	RYO	#	- FU
shiita*geru*	#	#	#	osore	#
r 141 s 9	r 141 s 11	r 61 s 15	r 141 s 13	r 141 s 13	r 130 s 15

　　■□　尸　尸　耂　方

尸	尺 *shaku*; measure SHAKU # r 44　s 4	尽 exhaust - JIN tsu*kusu*.. r 44*　s 6	昼 daytime, noon CHŪ hiru r 72　s 9	尼 nun - NI ama r 44　s 5	尾 tail - BI o r 44　s 7	尿 urine - NYŌ # r 44　s 7

届 deliver - todo*ku*.. r 44　s 8	屈 bend; yield KUTSU # r 44　s 8	局 bureau; local; state, condition KYOKU # r 44　s 7

居 reside, be present KYO *iru* r 44　s 8	屋 house; -seller OKU ya r 44　s 9	展 display, unfold TEN # r 44　s 10	属 belong - ZOKU # r 44　s 12	層 layer - SŌ # r 44　s 14	履 shoes; do RI ha*ku* r 44　s 15

民 the people - MIN tami r 83　s 5	刷 print - SATSU su*ru* r 18　s 8	尉 military officer I # r 41　s 11	殿 Mr, Mrs; palace DEN TEN tono -dono r 79　s 13

尸	戻 return - REI modo*ru*.. r 63　s 7	房 room; tassel BŌ fusa r 63　s 8	肩 shoulder - KEN kata r 130　s 8	扇 fan (folding, electric) SEN ōgi r 63　s 10	扉 door - HI tobira r 63　s 12	雇 employ - KO yato*u* r 172　s 12

戸 door - KO to r 63　s 4

耂	老 old age - RŌ o*iru* fu+ r 125　s 6	考 consider - KŌ kanga*eru* r 125　s 6	孝 filial piety KŌ # r 39　s 7	者 person - SHA mono r 125　s 8	煮 boil, cook SHA.. nie*ru*.. r 86　s 12

方	放 set free; emit HŌ hana*tsu*.. r 66　s 8	旅 travel - RYO tabi r 70　s 10	施 do; donate SHI SE hodoko*su* r 70　s 9	旋 rotation - SEN # r 70　s 11	族 family - ZOKU # r 70　s 11	旗 flag - KI hata r 70　s 14

厂 歹 戸

石
stone
-
SEKI SHAKU
ishi
r 112 s 5

死
death
-
SHI
shi*nu*
r 78 s 6

后
empress
-
KŌ
#
r 30 s 6

屮 产 产

皮
skin
-
HI
kawa
r 107 s 5

危
dangerous
-
KI
abu*nai* aya+
r 26 s 6

産
give birth
-
SAN
ubu u+
r 100 s 11

业 羊

厳
severe
-
GEN GON
kibi*shii* ogoso+
r 27* s 17

差
difference
-
SA
sa*su*
r 48 s 10

着
arrive;
wear, clothes
CHAKU JAKU
ki*ru.*. tsu+
r 109* s 12

丰 手

寿
longevity
-
JU
kotobuki
r 41* s 7

看
watch over
-
KAN
#
r 109 s 9

夕 尹

名
name;
fame
MEI MYŌ
na
r 30 s 6

多
many
-
TA
ō*i*
r 36 s 6

君
lord;
you
KUN
kimi
r 30 s 7

耳 昻 令

取
take
-
SHU
to*ru*
r 29 s 8

最
utmost
-
SAI
motto*mo*
r 72* s 12

倉
warehouse
-
SŌ
kura
r 9 s 10

1	33
2	34
3	35
4	36
5	37
6	38
7	39
8	40
9	41
10	42
11	43
12	44
13	45
14	46
15	47
16	48
17	49
18	50
19	51
20	52
21	53
22	54
23	55
24	**56**
25	57
26	58
27	59
28	60
29	61
30	62
31	63
32	64

迚

送	速	連	逮	進
take turns	quick	linked; series	capture	advance
-	-	-	-	-
TETSU	SOKU	REN	TAI	SHIN
#	haya*i*.. sumi+	tsu*reru* tsura+		susu*mu*..
r 162 s 8	r 162 s 10	r 162 s 10	r 162 s 11	r 162 s 11

込	辺	逐	退	遇
crowded; enter, insert	vicinity	expel; in turn	retreat	meet; deal with
#	HEN	CHIKU	TAI	GŪ
ko*mu*..	ata*ri* -be	#	shirizo*ku*..	#
r 162 s 5	r 162 s 5	r 162 s 10	r 162 s 9	r 162 s 12

述	迷	迫	追
say	astray, lost	press, urge; approach	chase; expel
-	-	-	-
JUTSU	MEI	HAKU	TSUI
no*beru*	mayo*u*	sema*ru*	o*u*
r 162 s 8	r 162 s 9	r 162 s 8	r 162 s 9

迚

迎	逃	進
welcome	escape	advance
-	-	-
GEI	TŌ	SHIN
muka*eru*	ni*geru*.. noga+	susu*mu*..
r 162 s 7	r 162 s 9	r 162 s 11

逝	避	遊	巡
die, death	evade	fun, play; tour	patrol, tour
SEI	-	YŪ YU	JUN
yu*ku*	HI	aso*bu*	megu*ru*
r 162 s 10	sa*keru*	r 162 s 12	r 47 s 6
	r 162 s 16		

迚

近	返	遮	遍	遅	逓
near; recent	return, repay	obstruct	widespread	slow; delayed	relay; in turn
KIN	HEN	-	-	CHI	TEI
chika*i*	kae*ru*..	SHA	HEN	oso*i* oku+	#
r 162 s 7	r 162 s 7	saegi*ru*			
		r 162 s 14	r 162 s 12	r 162 s 12	r 162 s 10

迚

迅
quick
-
JIN
#
r 162 s 6

迚

週	過	適
week	exceed; err	suitable
-		-
SHŪ	KA	TEKI
#	su*giru*.. ayama+	#
r 162 s 11	r 162 s 12	r 162 s 14

辶 迂

迫	追	述
press, urge; approach HAKU sema*ru* r 162 s 8	chase; expel TSUI o*u* r 162 s 9	say - JUTSU no*beru* r 162 s 8

迷	送	逆	遂	道	遵
astray, lost MEI mayo*u* r 162 s 9	send - SŌ oku*ru* r 162 s 9	inverse; counter- GYAKU saka saka+ r 162 s 9	accomplish - SUI to*geru* r 162 s 12	way, road DŌ TŌ michi r 162 s 12	comply - JUN # r 162 s 15

造	遺	遣	違	遠	達
make - ZŌ tsuku*ru* r 162 s 10	bequeath - I YUI # r 162 s 15	send; spend; use KEN tsuka*u..* r 162 s 13	differ; disobey I chiga*u..* r 162 s 13	distant - EN ON tō*i* r 162 s 13	achieve - TATSU # r 162 s 12

適	逮	遭
suitable - TEKI # r 162 s 14	capture - TAI # r 162 s 11	encounter - SŌ a*u* r 162 s 14

逸	途	透
miss, let slip; deviate; excel ITSU # r 162 s 11	way - TO # r 162 s 10	transparent - TŌ su*ku..* r 162 s 10

遍	遷	還	運	通
widespread - HEN # r 162 s 12	transition - SEN # r 162 s 15	return - KAN # r 162 s 16	transport; luck UN hako*bu* r 162 s 12	pass; street; commute; … TSŪ TSU tō*ru..* kayo+ r 162 s 10

選	導
select - SEN era*bu* r 162 s 15	guide - DŌ michibi*ku* r 41 s 15

ㄙ　廴　走

廴

廷
law court
-
TEI
#
r 54　s 7

延
prolong;
postpone
EN
no*basu*..
r 54　s 8

建
build
-
KEN KON
ta*teru*..
r 54　s 9

走

赴
go to
-
FU
omomu*ku*
r 156　s 9

起
wake up,
rise; begin
KI
o*kiru*..
r 156　s 10

超
surpass
-
CHŌ
ko*su*..
r 156　s 12

趣
gist; motive;
elegance
SHŪ
omomuki
r 156　s 15

越
exceed
-
ETSU
ko*su*..
r 156　s 12

■

直	置	断	県
directly; fix	put, place	sever; decide	prefecture
CHOKU JIKI	CHI	DAN	KEN
nao*su*.. tada+	*oku*	kotowa*ru* ta+	#
r 109 s 8	r 122 s 13	r 69 s 11	r 109* s 9

処	題
deal with	title, topic
-	
SHO	DAI
#	#
r 16* s 5	r 181 s 18

勉	魅
diligent; strive	enchant
-	-
BEN	MI
#	#
r 19 s 10	r 194 s 15

寸 tiny - SUN # r 41 s 3	可 possible; approve KA # r 30 s 5	司 official; officiate SHI # r 30 s 5	奇 strange - KI # r 37 s 8	寄 approach; give KI yoru.. r 40 s 11	
勺 *shaku* - SHAKU # r 20 s 3	句 phrase - KU # r 30 s 5	旬 10 day period JUN SHUN # r 72 s 6	包 wrap - HŌ tsutsumu r 20 s 5	匁 *monme* - # monme r 20 s 4	
式 rite; style SHIKI # r 56 s 6	弐 two - NI # r 56* s 6	武 military - BU MU # r 77 s 8	戒 warn; command KAI imashimeru r 62 s 7	我 I, my; self; selfish GA ware wa r 62 s 7	
成 become; consist of SEI JŌ naru.. r 62 s 6	威 power; threat I # r 38 s 9	栽 plant - SAI # r 75 s 10	載 load; publish SAI noru.. r 159 s 13	裁 judge; cut SAI sabaku ta+ r 145 s 12	幾 how many - KI iku r 52 s 12
飛 fly, jump HI tobu.. r 183 s 9	鳥 bird - CHŌ tori r 196 s 11	島 island - TŌ shima r 46 s 10			
斗 ladle; *to* TO # r 68 s 4	以 by means of; datum I # r 9 s 5	少 few - SHŌ sukoshi suku+ r 42 s 4			

区
district, ward
KU
#
r 22* s 4

匹
comparable
-
HITSU
hiki
r 22* s 4

巨
huge
-
KYO
#
r 48 s 5

臣
vassal, retainer
SHIN JIN
#
r 131 s 7

医
doctor; medical
I
#
r 22* s 7

匠
craftsman
-
SHŌ
#
r 22 s 6

匿
conceal
-
TOKU
#
r 22* s 10

枢
pivotal
-
SŪ
#
r 75 s 8

駆
spur on; drive; expel
KU
ka*ru..*
r 187 s 14

冠
crown
-
KAN
kanmuri
r 14 s 9

鬼
demon; ghost
KI
oni
r 194 s 10

凶
misfortune; evil
KYŌ
#
r 17 s 4

山
mountain
-
SAN
yama
r 46 s 3

出
go out, exit; put out
SHUTSU SUI
de*ru* da+
r 17 s 5

画
picture; *kanji* stroke
GA KAKU
#
r 102 s 8

幽
deep; hidden; remote; …
YŪ
#
r 52 s 9

歯
tooth
-
SHI
ha
r 77* s 12

凹
concave, hollow
-
Ō
#
r 17 s 5

凸
concave
-
TOTSU
#
r 17 s 5

1	33
2	34
3	35
4	36
5	37
6	38
7	39
8	40
9	41
10	42
11	43
12	44
13	45
14	46
15	47
16	48
17	49
18	50
19	51
20	52
21	53
22	54
23	55
24	56
25	57
26	58
27	**59**
28	60
29	61
30	62
31	63
32	64

冂 刀 几 門

同	円	内	肉	向	尚
same	circle; yen	inside	meat, flesh	facing	respect; valued
-	EN	-	NIKU	KŌ	SHŌ
DŌ	marui	NAI DAI	#	mukau..	#
onaji	r 13* s 4	uchi	r 130 s 6	r 30 s 6	r 42 s 8
r 30 s 6		r 13* s 4			

周	丹	舟	用	月
circum-ference	vermilion; sincerely	boat	task; use, employ	month; moon; Monday
SHŪ	TAN	-	YŌ	GETSU GATSU
mawari	#	SHŪ	mochiiru	tsuki
r 30 s 8	r 3 s 4	fune funa-	r 101 s 5	r 74 s 4
		r 137 s 6		

凡	風
ordinary	wind; style
-	FŪ FU
BON HAN	kaze kaza-
#	r 182 s 9
r 16 s 3	

問	間	聞	閑	閉	開
question	interval	hear, listen; ask	leisure	closed	open
-	-	BUN MON	-	-	-
MON	KAN KEN	kiku..	KAN	HEI	KAI
toi.. ton	aida ma	r 128 s 14	#	shimeru.. to+	akeru.. hira+
r 30 s 11	r 169 s 12		r 169 s 12	r 169 s 11	r 169 s 12

関	閲	閣	閥	闘
barrier; connected	review	tower; cabinet	clique	fight
KAN	-	KAKU	-	-
seki	ETSU	#	BATSU	TŌ
r 169 s 14	#	r 169 s 14	#	tatakau
	r 169 s 15		r 169 s 14	r 169* s 18

簡	門
simple, brief	gate, door
KAN	MON
#	kado
r 118 s 18	r 169 s 8

关

券	巻
ticket	roll; scroll; book
-	
KEN	KAN
#	maki ma+
r 18 s 8	r 49* s 9

夫

奉	春	奏	泰
offering; respectful	springtime	play music	tranquil
HŌ BU	-	-	-
tatematsuru	SHUN	SŌ	TAI
	haru	kanaderu	#
r 37 s 8	r 72 s 9	r 37 s 9	r 85 s 10

…

太	冬	寒	寿	為	参
thick; great	winter	cold	longevity	do; purpose	visit; join in
TA TAI	-	-	-	I	SAN
futoi..	TŌ	KAN	JU	#	mairu
	fuyu	samui	kotobuki		
r 37 s 4	r 15* s 5	r 40 s 12	r 41* s 7	r 86* s 9	r 28 s 8

尽	昼	局
exhaust	daytime, noon	bureau; local; state, condition
-	CHŪ	KYOKU
JIN	hiru	#
tsukusu..		
r 44* s 6	r 72 s 9	r 44 s 7

威	蔵	繭	雨
power; threat	store, keep	cocoon	rain
I	ZŌ	-	-
#	kura	KEN	U
		mayu	ame ama-
r 38 s 9	r 140 s 15	r 120 s 18	r 173 s 8

何	伺	河	筒	荷
what, how many	visit; pay respects	river	tube	load, cargo
KA	SHI	-	-	KA
nani nan	ukagau	KA	TŌ	ni
		kawa	tsutsu	
r 9 s 7	r 9 s 7	r 85 s 8	r 118 s 12	r 140 s 10

高	商	南
high, tall; sum	trade	south
KŌ	-	-
taka taka+	SHŌ	NAN NA
	akinau	minami
r 189 s 10	r 30 s 11	r 24 s 9

1	33
2	34
3	35
4	36
5	37
6	38
7	39
8	40
9	41
10	42
11	43
12	44
13	45
14	46
15	47
16	48
17	49
18	50
19	51
20	52
21	53
22	54
23	55
24	56
25	57
26	58
27	59
28	**60**
29	61
30	62
31	63
32	64

囚	因	困	田	四
prisoner	cause	suffer; trouble	rice field	four
-	-	KON	-	SHI
SHŪ	IN	komaru	DEN	yo yo+ yo'+ yon
#	yoru		ta	
r 31 s 5	r 31 s 6	r 31 s 7	r 102 s 5	r 31 s 5

回	団	図	囲	国
turn, rotate; times	group, body	diagram	encircle	country
KAI E	DAN TON	ZU TO	-	KOKU
mawasu	#	hakaru	I	kuni
			kakomu..	
r 31 s 6	r 31 s 6	r 31 s 7	r 31 s 7	r 31 s 8

固	園	圏
firm, hard	gardens	sphere
KO	-	KEN
katai..	EN	#
	sono	
r 31 s 8	r 31 s 13	r 31 s 12

口	日	目
mouth	day; Japan; sun; Sunday	eye; -th
-	NICHI JITSU	-
KŌ KU	hi -ka	MOKU BOKU
kuchi		me ma-
r 30 s 3	r 72 s 4	r 109 s 5

丹	舟	母	箇	菌
vermilion; sincerely	boat	mother	item	germ; fungi
TAN	-	-	-	KIN
#	SHŪ	BO	KA	#
	fune funa-	haha	#	
r 3 s 4	r 137 s 6	r 80 s 5	r 118 s 14	r 140 s 11

術	街	衝	衛	衡
art, skill	street, arcade	collide	guard	balance, scales
-	-	-	-	-
JUTSU	GAI KAI	SHŌ	EI	KŌ
#	machi	#	#	#
r 60* s 11	r 60* s 12	r 60* s 15	r 60* s 16	r 60* s 16

問	間	聞	閑	閉	開
question	interval	hear, listen; ask	leisure	closed	open
MON	KAN KEN	BUN MON	KAN	HEI	KAI
to*i..* ton	aida ma	ki*ku..*	#	shi*meru..* to+	a*keru..* hira+
r 30 s 11	r 169 s 12	r 128 s 14	r 169 s 12	r 169 s 11	r 169 s 12

関	閲	閣	閥	闘
barrier; connected	review	tower; cabinet	clique	fight
KAN	ETSU	KAKU	BATSU	TŌ
seki	#	#	#	tataka*u*
r 169 s 14	r 169 s 15	r 169 s 14	r 169 s 14	r 169* s 18

班	承	門	簡	行
squad	consent; be told	gate, door	simple, brief	go; do; line
-	-	-	-	-
HAN	SHŌ	MON	KAN	GYŌ KŌ AN
#	uketamawa*ru*	kado	#	*iku* yu+ okona+
r 96 s 10	r 64 s 8	r 169 s 8	r 118 s 18	r 144 s 6

疑	務	能	殺
doubt	duties	ability; *Noh* play	kill
-	-		
GI	MU	NŌ	SATSU SETSU SAI
utaga*u*	tsuto*meru*	#	koro*su*
r 103 s 14	r 19 s 11	r 130 s 10	r 79 s 10

競	鼓	殻	穀	行
compete	drum	shell	grain, cereal	go; do; line
-	-	-	-	
KYŌ KEI	KO	KAKU	KOKU	GYŌ KŌ AN
kiso*u* se+	tsuzumi	kara	#	*iku* yu+ okona+
r 117 s 20	r 207 s 13	r 79 s 11	r 115 s 14	r 144 s 6

辞	韻	静	解	齢
word; resign	rhyme, tone	quiet	unravel; solve	age
JI	IN	-	KAI GE	-
ya*meru*	#	SEI JŌ	to*ku..*	REI
r 160 s 13	r 180 s 19	shizu shizu+	r 148 s 13	#
		r 174 s 14		r 211 s 17

For ⊞ see also 言 on page 14 and ⺶ on page 41.

1	33
2	34
3	35
4	36
5	37
6	38
7	39
8	40
9	41
10	42
11	43
12	44
13	45
14	46
15	47
16	48
17	49
18	50
19	51
20	52
21	53
22	54
23	55
24	56
25	57
26	58
27	59
28	60
29	**61**
30	62
31	63
32	64

十	土	士	止	上	
ten	soil, land; Saturday	warrior; man	stop	above, up	
-	-	-	-	-	
JŪ JI'	DO TO	SHI	SHI	JŌ SHŌ	
tō to	tsuchi	#	tomaru..	ue kami uwa- a+ nobo+	
r 24 s 2	r 32 s 3	r 33 s 3	r 77 s 4	r 1 s 3	

山	出	屯	亡	七	
mountain	go out, exit; put out	barracks	deceased	seven	
-	-	-	-	-	
SAN	SHUTSU SUI	TON	BŌ MŌ	SHICHI	
yama	deru da+	#	nai	nana nana+ nano	
r 46 s 3	r 17 s 5	r 45 s 4	r 8 s 3	r 1 s 2	

木	本	米	来	未	末
tree, wood; Thursday	book; this; base	rice; America	come	not yet	end
BOKU MOKU	HON	BEI MAI	-	MI	MATSU BATSU
ki ko-	moto	kome	RAI	#	sue
r 75 s 4	r 75 s 5	r 119 s 6	kuru kita+	r 75 s 5	r 75 s 5
			r 75* s 7		

半	牛	朱	生		
half, semi-, pen-	cow, bull	vermilion	life; birth; grow; raw		
HAN	-	-	SHŌ SEI		
nakaba	GYŪ	SHU	nama i+ u+ ha+ o+ ki-		
r 24 s 5	ushi	#	r 100 s 5		
	r 93 s 4	r 75 s 6			

斗	寸	才	与	皮	衣
ladle;	tiny	talent; years old	give	skin	garment
to	-	SAI	-	-	-
TO	SUN	#	YO	HI	I
#	#	r 64 s 3	ataeru	kawa	koromo
r 68 s 4	r 41 s 3		r 1* s 3	r 107 s 5	r 145 s 6

小	水	氷	永	求	
small	water; Wednesday	ice	eternal	seek, request	
-	SUI	-	-	KYŪ	
SHŌ	mizu	HYŌ	EI	motomeru	
chiisai ko- o-	r 85 s 4	kōri kō- hi	nagai	r 85 s 7	
r 42 s 3		r 85 s 5	r 85 s 5		

中	虫	束	事	肅	
middle; China	insect	bundle	thing, matter	solemn; purge	
CHŪ	-	-	JI ZU	SHUKU	
naka	CHŪ	SOKU	koto	#	
r 2 s 4	mushi	taba	r 6 s 8	r 129 s 11	
	r 142 s 6	r 75 s 7			

申	由	東	車		
say, report	reason, cause	east	vehicle		
SHIN	YU YŪ YUI	-	-		
mōsu	yoshi	TŌ	SHA		
r 102 s 5	r 102 s 5	higashi	kuruma		
		r 75 s 8	r 159 s 7		

止	片	甘	井	世	曲
stop	part, flake; single, one-	sweet	well (for water)	world; era	bend; melody
-	HEN	-	SEI SHŌ	SE SEI	KYOKU
SHI	kata	KAN	i	yo	ma*geru*..
to*maru*..	r 91 s 4	ama*i*..	r 7 s 4	r 1 s 5	r 72* s 6
r 77 s 4		r 99 s 5			

甚
extremely
-
JIN
hanaha*da*..
r 99 s 9

人	火	入	八
person	fire; Tuesday	enter; put in, let in	eight
-	KA	NYŪ	HACHI
JIN NIN	hi ho	ha*iru* i+	ya ya'+ ya+ yō
hito	r 86 s 4	r 11 s 2	r 12 s 2
r 9 s 2			

大	犬	太	夫	失	先
large	dog	thick; great	husband	lose; error	ahead; previous
-	-	TA TAI	FU FŪ	SHITSU	SEN
DAI TAI	KEN	futo*i*..	otto	ushina*u*	saki
ō- ō+	inu	r 37 s 4	r 37 s 4	r 37 s 5	r 10 s 6
r 37 s 3	r 94 s 4				

丈	史	吏	央
robust; height, stature	history	official	center
JŌ	SHI	RI	Ō
take	#	#	#
r 1 s 3	r 30 s 5	r 30 s 6	r 37 s 5

内	肉	力	丸	九
inside	meat, flesh	power	round	nine
-	NIKU	-	-	-
NAI DAI	#	RIKI RYOKU	GAN	KYŪ KU
uchi	r 130 s 6	chikara	-maru maru+	kokono kokono+
r 13* s 4		r 19 s 2	r 3 s 3	r 5 s 2

女	与	糸	寿
woman	give	thread	longevity
-	-	-	-
JO NYO NYŌ	YO	SHI	JU
onna me	ata*eru*	ito	kotobuki
r 38 s 3	r 1* s 3	r 120 s 6	r 41* s 7

一
one
-
ICHI ITSU
hito*tsu* hito-
r 1 s 1

丁
city block;
4th; ...
CHŌ TEI
#
r 1 s 2

工
industry;
worker
KŌ KU
#
r 48 s 3

不
not,
un-
FU BU
#
r 1 s 4

下
below,
down
KA GE
shita moto shimo sa+ o+ kuda+
r 1 s 3

干
dry
-
KAN
hi*ru* ho+
r 51 s 3

平
level;
calm
HEI BYŌ
hira tai+
r 51 s 5

王
king
-
Ō
#
r 96 s 4

玉
jewel
-
GYOKU
tama
r 96 s 5

正
correct
-
SHŌ SEI
tada*su*.. masa
r 77 s 5

五
five
-
GO
itsu itsu+
r 7 s 4

天
heaven,
sky
TEN
ame ama-
r 37 s 4

万
ten thousand;
many
MAN BAN
#
r 1* s 3

石
stone
-
SEKI SHAKU
ishi
r 112 s 5

死
death
-
SHI
shi*nu*
r 78 s 6

互
mutual
-
GO
taga*i*
r 7 s 4

丙
3rd
-
HEI
#
r 1 s 5

両
both
-
RYŌ
#
r 1* s 6

雨
rain
-
U
ame ama-
r 173 s 8

西
west
-
SEI SAI
nishi
r 146 s 6

亜
Asia;
sub-
A
#
r 7 s 7

耳
ear
-
JI
mimi
r 128 s 6

更
renew;
late
KŌ
sara fu+
r 72* s 7

再
again;
re-
SAI SA
futata*bi*
r 13 s 6

画
picture;
kanji stroke
GA KAKU
#
r 102* s 8

百
hundred
-
HYAKU
#
r 106 s 6

面
face,
mask
MEN
omote omo tsura
r 176 s 9

■ ❏

❏

巨 huge - KYO # r 48 s 5	臣 vassal, retainer SHIN JIN # r 131 s 7	匹 comparable - HITSU hiki r 22* s 4	民 the people - MIN tami r 83 s 5	長 long; chief CHŌ naga*i* r 168 s 8	馬 horse - BA uma ma r 187 s 10
又 again - # mata r 29 s 2	乙 2nd - OTSU # r 5 s 1	己 self - KI KO onore r 49 s 3	弓 bow, archery KYŪ yumi r 57 s 3	弔 mourn, condole CHŌ tomura*u* r 57 s 4	
刀 sword - TŌ katana r 18 s 2	刃 blade - JIN ha r 18 s 3	及 attain - KYŪ oyo*bu..* r 29 s 3	了 finish; understand RYŌ # r 6 s 2	子 child - SHI SU ko r 39 s 3	
口 mouth - KŌ KU kuchi r 30 s 3	日 day; Japan; sun, Sunday NICHI JITSU hi -ka r 72 s 4	目 eye; -th - MOKU BOKU me ma- r 109 s 5	且 moreover, besides # ka*tsu* r 1 s 5	皿 dish - # sara r 108 s 5	母 mother - BO haha r 80 s 5
田 rice field - DEN ta r 102 s 5	甲 1st; shell KŌ KAN # r 102 s 5	凸 convex - TOTSU # r 17 s 5	凹 concave, hollow Ō # r 17 s 5	四 four - SHI yo yo+ yo'+ yon r 31 s 5	
用 task; use, employ YŌ mochi*iru* r 101 s 5	冊 books - SATSU SAKU # r 13 s 5	円 circle; *yen* EN maru*i* r 13* s 4	丹 vermilion; sincerely TAN # r 3 s 4	月 month; moon; Monday GETSU GATSU tsuki r 74 s 4	

1	33
2	34
3	35
4	36
5	37
6	38
7	39
8	40
9	41
10	42
11	43
12	44
13	45
14	46
15	47
16	48
17	49
18	50
19	51
20	52
21	53
22	54
23	55
24	56
25	57
26	58
27	59
28	60
29	61
30	62
31	**63**
32	64

千	斤	斥	丘	氏
thousand	*kin*	repel	hill	family name
-	-	-	-	
SEN	KIN	SEKI	KYŪ	SHI
chi	#	#	oka	uji
r 24 s 3	r 69 s 4	r 69 s 5	r 1 s 5	r 83 s 4

乏	升	我	毛	手
scarcity; poverty	*sho*; measure	I, my; self; selfish	hair, fur	hand
BŌ	SHŌ	GA	MŌ	SHU
tobo*shii*	masu	ware wa	ke	te ta
r 4 s 4	r 24 s 4	r 62 s 7	r 82 s 4	r 64 s 4

垂	乗	重
droop	ride	heavy; layered
-	-	
SUI	JŌ	JŪ CHŌ
ta*reru*..	no*ru*..	omo*i* kasa+ -e
r 32 s 8	r 4 s 9	r 166 s 9

午	矢	年	缶	々
noon	arrow	year	tin can	ditto (see footnote)
-	-	-	-	#
GO	SHI	NEN	KAN	#
#	ya	toshi	#	r - s -
r 24 s 4	r 111 s 5	r 51 s 6	r 121 s 6	

勺	夕	久	匁	欠
shaku	evening	long time	*monme*	lack
-	-	-	#	-
SHAKU	SEKI	KYŪ KU	#	KETSU
#	yu	hisa*shii*	monme	ka*ku*..
r 20 s 3	r 36 s 3	r 4 s 3	r 20 s 4	r 76 s 4

々 indicates duplication of the kanji it follows, and takes its reading from that kanji (sometimes the reading is slightly modified).

■   …

…

入	八	心	必	父

入
enter;
put in, let in
NYŪ
hairu i+
r 11 s 2

八
eight
-
HACHI
ya ya'+ ya+ yō
r 12 s 2

心
heart
-
SHIN
kokoro
r 61 s 4

必
inevitable
-
HITSU
kanarazu
r 61 s 5

父
father
-
FU
chichi
r 88 s 4

升
sho;
measure
SHŌ
masu
r 24 s 4

我
I, my; self;
selfish
GA
ware wa
r 62 s 7

飛
fly,
jump
HI
tobu..
r 183 s 9

為
do;
purpose
I
#
r 86* s 9

幽
deep; hidden;
remote; …
YŪ
#
r 52 s 9

○
zero
(see footnote)
REI
zero maru
r - s -

○ Is not officially a kanji but is used with Japanese numerals, for example in telephone numbers.

1	33
2	34
3	35
4	36
5	37
6	38
7	39
8	40
9	41
10	42
11	43
12	44
13	45
14	46
15	47
16	48
17	49
18	50
19	51
20	52
21	53
22	54
23	55
24	56
25	57
26	58
27	59
28	60
29	61
30	62
31	63
32	**64**

Table 1: Radicals

This table lists the traditional radicals: there are 214 in all, but some (omitted here) are not used among the *jōyō* kanji. The numbers in this table are the radical numbers used in the Fast Finder (and are fairly universally agreed). Some radicals are slightly distorted when appearing as parts of kanji; and you will see that some of the radicals have several different forms. Some older forms not used in the modern *jōyō* kanji have been omitted.

1	一	24	十	49	己	72	日
2	丨	25	卜	50	巾	73	曰
3	丶	26	卩 巳	51	干	74	月
4	丿 亅	27	厂	52	幺	75	木
5	乙 乚	28	厶	53	广	76	欠
6	亅	29	又	54	廴	77	止
7	二	30	口	55	廾	78	歹
8	亠	31	囗	56	弋	79	殳
9	人 𠆢 亻	32	土	57	弓	80	母 毋 毌
10	儿	33	士	58	彐 彑	81	比
11	入	34	夂	59	彡	82	毛
12	丷 八 八	35	夊	60	彳	83	氏
13	冂 冂	36	夕	61	心 忄 忄	84	气
14	冖	37	大	62	戈	85	水 氺 氵
15	冫	38	女	63	戸	86	火 灬
16	几 几	39	子	64	手 扌	87	爪 爫
17	凵	40	宀	65	支	88	父
18	刀 刂	41	寸	66	攵	90	爿
19	力	42	小 ⺌ ⺍	67	文	91	片
20	勹	44	尸	68	斗	92	牙
21	匕	46	山	69	斤	93	牛
22	匚	47	川 巛	70	方	94	犬 犭
23	匚 匸	48	工	71	无	95	玄

Table 1: Radicals (continued)

96	玉	王	124	羽		150	谷	
98	瓦		125	老	耂	151	豆	
99	甘		126	而		152	豸	
100	生		127	耒		154	貝	
101	用		128	耳		155	赤	
102	田		129	聿	肀	156	走	
103	疋	疋	130	肉	月	157	足	𧾷
104	疒		131	臣		158	身	
105	癶		132	自		159	車	
106	白		133	至		160	辛	
107	皮		134	臼		161	辰	
108	皿		135	舌		162	辶	
109	目		136	舛		163	阝	
110	矛		137	舟		164	酉	
111	矢		138	艮	艮	165	釆	
112	石		139	色		166	里	
113	示	礻	140	艹		167	金	
115	禾		141	虍		168	長	
116	穴	穴	142	虫		169	門	
117	立		143	血		170	阝	
118	竹	𥫗	144	行		172	隹	
119	米		145	衣	衤	173	雨	
120	糸		146	西	襾	174	青	
121	缶		147	見		175	非	
122	罒		148	角		176	面	
123	羊	羊	149	言		177	革	

180	音		
181	頁		
182	風		
183	飛		
184	食	飠
185	首	
186	香	
187	馬	
188	骨	
189	高	
190	髟	
191	鬥	
193	鬲	
194	鬼	
195	魚	
196	鳥	
198	鹿	
199	麦	
200	麻	
201	黄	
203	黒	
207	鼓	
209	鼻	
210	斉	
211	歯	
212	龍	竜

Table 2: Non-Traditional Radicals

The radical given in the Fast Finder is that used in the 'New Nelson' and 'Compact Nelson' kanji dictionaries[1]. In most cases this is the traditional historical radical. Where not, the radical number has an asterisk, and the kanji appears in the table below

The table gives the traditional radical and for comparison (where differing from the traditional radical) the radical associated with the kanji in Halpern[2] and in 'Classic' editions (up to 1997) of Nelson. In many cases, the reason that these kanji are allocated a non-traditional radical is that in the course of the kanji being gradually modified and simplified down the centuries, the original radical has undergone (sometimes drastic) modification or has even disappeared entirely.

New Nel.		Trad.	Halp.	Classic Nel.	New Nel.		Trad.	Halp.	Classic Nel.	New Nel.		Trad.	Halp.	Classic Nel.
1	万	140	1	1	29	叙	66	29	29	72	曲	73		72
1	与	134	1	1	30	台	133	30	28	72	更	73		72
1	並	117	1	12	30	号	141	30	30	72	最	73		72
1	両	11	1	1	30	営	86	42	30	72	曹	73		72
2	衷	145		2	32	声	128	33	32	72	書	73		72
6	予	152	6	6	32	売	154	33	32	72	替	73		72
6	争	87	6	4	32	壱	33		32	75	来	9	75	4
9	体	188	9	9	32	壮	33		32	75	巣	47	42	3
9	全	11	9	9	32	塩	197	32	32	77	歯	211		
9	会	73		9	34	夏	35	35	1	86	為	87	86	3
9	舎	135	9	9	34	変	149	34	8	86	点	203	86	25
9	舗	135	9	9	41	寿	33	41	3	109	冒	13	109	72
10	党	203	10	42	44	尽	108	44	44	109	県	120	109	42
13	内	11	13	2	49	巻	26	49	49	109	着	123		
13	円	31	13	13	50	帰	77	18	58	117	竜	212		
14	写	40	14	14	56	弐	154		1	130	服	74		130
16	処	141	16	34	58	当	102	42	42	130	朕	74		130
22	区	23		22	60	術	144		60	130	朗	74		130
22	匹	23		22	60	街	144		60	130	期	74		130
22	医	164	23	22	60	衝	144		60	130	朝	74		130
22	匿	23		22	60	衛	144		60	130	有	74		130
24	単	30	42	3	60	衡	144		60	130	望	74		130
27	厳	30	42	4	67	斉	210			169	闘	191	169	169
29	双	172	29	29	67	斎	210			181	頼	154		181
29	収	66	29	29	72	旧	134	72	2					

[1]   A.N. Nelson: *The Modern Reader's Japanese-English Character Dictionary*, Tuttle, Tokyo & Rutland, Vermont, revised edn. 1997; compact edn. abridged by J.H. Haig, 1999.

[2]   J. Halpern, *New Japanese-English Character Dictionary*, Kenkyusha, Tokyo, 1990.